C++

A Book and Disk Guide
for C Programmers

CW00725560

C++

A Book and Disk Guide
for C Programmers

Dr Sharam Hekmatpour
University of Melbourne

PRENTICE HALL

New York London Toronto Sydney Tokyo Singapore

Printed and bound in Singapore by
Fong & Sons Printers Pte Ltd
Cover desigy by Kim Webber.

3 4 5 94 93 92 91

0-13-174129-2

National Library of Australia
Cataloguing-in-Publication Data

Hekmatpour, Sharam, 1961 -
    C++, a book and disk guide for C programmers

    Bibliography
    Includes index.
    ISBN: 0-13-174129-2

    1. C++ (Computer program language). I. Title.

005.133

Library of Congress
Cataloguing-in-Publication Data

Hekmatpour, Sharam, 1961-
    C++ : a book and disk guide for C programmers

    Includes bibliographical references.
    1. C++ (Computer program language) I. Title.

QA76.73.C153H45   1990   005.26   90-6936
ISBN 0-13-174129-2

Prentice Hall, Inc., *Englewood Cliffs, New Jersey*
Prentice Hall Canada, Inc., *Toronto*
Prentice Hall Hispanoamericana, SA, *Mexico*
Prentice Hall of India Private Ltd, *New Delhi*
Prentice Hall International, Inc., *London*
Prentice Hall of Japan, Inc., *Tokyo*
Prentice Hall of Southeast Asia Pty Ltd, *Singapore*
Editora Prentice Hall do Brasil Ltda, *Rio de Janeiro*

PRENTICE HALL

A division of Simon & Schuster

Contents

Preface

The ever-increasing popularity of object-oriented programming [Verity 1987] in recent years has lead to the appearance of a number of programming languages aimed at supporting it. C++ is one such language. Developed by Bjarne Stroustrup [1986] at the AT&T Bell Laboratories, C++ supports proper data abstraction and encapsulation, making it an attractive programming language for the development of large and complex software systems. Because it is a superset of the C programming language, it can be quickly mastered by C programmers.

The aim of this book is to introduce C programmers to those facilities of C++ that are not available in C. A reasonable working knowledge of C is therefore assumed. The book is suitable for undergraduate/graduate students in science and engineering who have already done some C programming, as well as C programmers in industry.

The book is divided into two parts. The first part consists of Chapters 1-9, which describe the facilities of C++ in detail. Each chapter introduces one major facility, which is subsequently illustrated by examples. The reader is strongly encouraged to try the examples and to also attempt the exercises. Sample solutions to most exercises are provided in an appendix.

Chapter 1 introduces the class construct and describes the way C++ programs are organized and compiled. Chapter 2 describes constructors and destructors – two specific type of member functions, which implicitly create and destroy objects of a class. Chapter 3 illustrates the use of friends; these allow access to the private part of a class by nonmember functions. The overloading of functions and operators is discussed in Chapter 4, which also describes user-defined type conversion rules. Chapter 5 looks at the use of references and compares them to pointers. Chapter 6 describes how new classes are derived from existing ones. Chapter 7 distinguishes between single and multiple inheritance, discussing the latter in some detail. Issues related to the use of pointers and dynamically allocated blocks are discussed in Chapter 8. Chapter 9 describes the remaining features of C++, including structures, generic classes, and library-supported I/O facilities.

The second part of the book, Chapters 10-14, describes four relatively large case studies. The case studies are self-contained and offer solutions to some nontrivial problems. The aim of the studies is to illustrate the way C++ is used as an object-oriented programming language. The reader is advised to attempt these studies only after a good knowledge of the language has been attained.

Chapter 10 describes the implementation of a B-tree and its variants as classes. The derived class developed in this chapter illustrates a typical use of virtual functions. Chapter 11 describes the implementation of a memory management algorithm which is later extended by a derived class to include relocatable blocks. Chapter 12 applies the facilities of C++ to the design of a window-based user interface manager. This is implemented as four classes. Chapter 13 illustrates the use of multiple inheritance by presenting a hierarchy of 8 classes for a word processing application.

The C++ examples, solutions, and code fragments appearing in this book have all been compiled and tested using the public domain GNU C++ compiler [Tiemann 1989]. Use of implementation-specific facilities has, so far as possible, been avoided.

Acknowledgments

I am grateful to Justin Zobel and Michael Fisher for reading an earlier draft of this book and making a number of useful suggestions. I am also debted to Peter Poole, David Spaziani, Timothy Leask, and Michael Paddon for their help and encouragement.

Sharam   Hekmatpour

Classes

This chapter introduces the class construct of C++ for defining new data types. The main components of a class definition are explained using some simple examples. The examples also illustrate how the new facilities of C++, such as enum, const and inline, can be used instead of C macros to improve readability. Finally, compilation and arrangement of C++ programs is discussed.

1.1 Introduction

Programs written in C and similar conventional languages invariably consist of a collection of data structures and a set of routines that manipulate them. Because such languages offer no data abstraction facilities, it is usually unclear by which routines a data structure is manipulated. Furthermore, the language has no way of preventing access to a data structure by routines that are not intended to have such access. As a result, large programs become unnecessarily complicated and many accidental design errors may go unnoticed.

Use of a programming language that offers facilities for the encapsulation and abstraction of data structures, and their associated operations, can have a significant influence upon the way programs are designed. It encourages the programmer to investigate the problem domain much more carefully, untangling dependencies that may otherwise seem necessary. The result is programs that consist of self-contained units (called **data types**) that have simple and well-defined interfaces.

The **class** construct is the most important addition of C++ to C. It provides the programmer with a simple and powerful tool for defining new data types. A data type consists of two things:

- a concrete representation of the objects of the type, and
- a set of operations for manipulating the objects.

Added to these is the restriction that – other than the designated operations – no other operation should be able to manipulate the objects. For this reason, we often say that the operations *characterize* the type, that is, they decide what can and what cannot happen to the objects. For the same reason, proper data types as such are often called **abstract data types** – abstract because the internal representation of the objects is hidden from operations that do not belong to the type.

All useful programming languages contain a number of built-in data types. For example, floating point numbers together with the 4 arithmetic operations of addition, subtraction, multiplication, and division represent a common built-in data type. What distinguishes C++ from many other languages is the ability to define new data types in a way that their use cannot be distinguished from the built-in types. In this way, a program (or at least a part of it) becomes a natural extension of the language rather than something separate from it.

Three important benefits make the use of proper data types attractive. Firstly, programs written in this style are easier to understand and to modify, because the overall complexity of the program is significantly reduced. Secondly, many accidental design errors can be avoided. Since the objects of a data type can be manipulated only through their own private operations, errors are readily localized. Finally, because each data type is a self-contained entity independent of others, the design task can be broken down into a number of subtasks that can be carried out in isolation. This ability is essential in large systems that involve many designers and programmers.

1.2 The class construct

In C++, new data types are defined using the `class` construct. The syntax of a `class` declaration is similar to that of a C `struct` declaration, except that the former can also contain function declarations. For example,

```
class Point {
     int xVal, yVal;
public:
     void SetPt (int,int);
     void OffsetPt (int,int);
};
```

declares a new class called `Point`. It contains two data members (`xVal` and `yVal`) and two function members (`SetPt` and `OffsetPt`). The four components are collectively called **members** of the class. `Point` consists of two parts: a **private** part and a **public** part. These two are separated by the keyword `public`. Members appearing in the private part can be accessed by the function members only. Members appearing in the public part can be accessed by a user of the class. The public part, in other words, specifies an **interface** to the class.

The implementation of a function member is usually not part of the class and appears separately (but see `inline` below). For example, `SetPt` and `OffsetPt` may be defined as:

```
void Point::SetPt (int x, int y)
{
    xVal = x;
    yVal = y;
}


void Point::OffsetPt (int x, int y)
{
    xVal += x;
    yVal += y;
}
```

In these definitions, the name of each function member is preceded by `Point::` to indicate which class it belongs to. This avoids any ambiguity when different classes have function members with identical names. The function members have free access to the private part of the class: both `SetPt` and `OffsetPt` refer to `xVal` and `yVal` from the private part of `Point`.

Once a class is defined in this way, its name denotes a new data type, allowing us to define variables of that type.[1]

```
Point pt;                 // pt is an object in class Point
pt.SetPt(10,20);          // pt is set to (10,20)
pt.OffsetPt(2,2);         // pt becomes (12,22)
```

Function members are called using the dot notation: `pt.SetPt(10,20)` calls `SetPt` for the object pt, that is, pt is an *implicit* argument to `SetPt`.

By including `xVal` and `yVal` in the private part of the class, we have ensured that a user of the class cannot manipulate them directly.

---

[1] In addition to the C notation for writing comments (i.e., `/*...*/`), in C++, anything appearing after a `//` until the end of the line is a comment.

```
pt.xVal = 10;                    // illegal
```

This will not compile. So if at some stage an object of type `Point` misbehaves, we know where to look for the source of the error; it has to be one of the function members. C has no means of imposing such restrictions. If something goes wrong, the source of the error may not be obvious, especially when the program is large and contains many subtle interconnections.

At this stage, we should clearly distinguish between object and class. A class denotes a type, of which there is only one. An object is an element of a particular type (class), of which there may be many. For example,

```
Point pt1, pt2, pt3;
```

defines three objects (`pt1`, `pt2`, and `pt3`) all of the same class (`Point`). Furthermore, operations of a class are applied to objects of that class, but never the class itself. A class is therefore a concept that has no concrete existence other than that reflected by its objects.

1.3 Inline functions

Every operation of a class is realized by a function member, and the use of that operation represents a function call. While the overheads of a function call are acceptable for relatively large operations, for small and frequently used operations these can be too prohibitive. This problem is overcome by defining such functions to be **inline**. This causes the code for the function to be inserted in the place of every call to the function (in a way that will preserve its semantics), thereby avoiding the overheads of the function call mechanism.

In the class `Point`, both function members are very short (only two statements). Defining these to be inline improves the efficiency considerably. A function can be defined to be inline by inserting the keyword `inline` before its definition.

```
inline void Point::SetPt (int x, int y)
{
    xVal = x;
    yVal = y;
}
```

Any function can be inline, including global functions (i.e., functions that are not members of any class). For a function member, an easier way of defining it to be inline is to include its definition inside the class.

```
class Point {
    int xVal, yVal;
public:
    void SetPt (int x, int y)      { xVal = x; yVal = y; }
    void OffsetPt (int x, int y)   { xVal += x; yVal += y; }
};
```

1.4 Example: a set implementation

A set is an unordered collection of objects. Using the class construct, we would
like to define set as a new data type. For simplicity, we restrict ourselves to sets of
integers with a finite number of elements. Given this restriction, a set can be
implemented as a static array of integers. We also have to record the number of
elements in a set at (i.e., its cardinality).[2]

```
class Set {
    int elems[maxCard];        // set elements
    int card;                  // set cardinality
public:
    void     EmptySet ()       { card = 0; }
    Bool     Member (int);
    ErrCode  AddElem (int);
    void     RmvElem (int);
    void     Copy (Set*);
    Bool     Equal (Set*);
    void     Print ();
    void     Intersect (Set*, Set*);
    ErrCode  Union (Set*, Set*);
};
```

MaxCard denotes the maximum number of elements a set may have. This is
defined as a constant. In C++ (and ANSI C), constants are defined using the const
construct; this is preferred over the use of #define.

```
const maxCard = 16;        // similar to: #define maxCard 16
```

Some of the function members in Set return a Bool or ErrCode result. These two
are defined as enumerations.

```
enum Bool { false, true };
enum ErrCode { noErr, overflow };
```

---

[2] There are better ways of defining a set. These are described in subsequent chapters.

The effect of these two lines is the same as:

```
const false    = 0;
const true     = 1;
const noErr    = 0;
const overflow = 1;
```

The advantage of using an enumeration is improved readability; the name introduced by an enum can be used as a type name in the rest of the program. The name, however, does not introduce a new type, but rather a synonym for int. So both Bool and ErrCode above become aliases for int. (For a more detailed description of constants and enumerations see Section 9.1.)

The first function member, EmptySet, is straightforward and is defined inline. It simply sets the cardinality of a set to zero. The second function member, Member, checks if a given integer is an element of a set.

```
Bool Set::Member (int elem)      // test if elem is a member of set
{
    for (int i = 0; i < card; ++i)
        if (elems[i] == elem)
            return true;
    return false;
} /* Member */
```

Note the way the local variable i is declared inside the for-loop, rather than outside it. In C++, a variable declaration may appear anywhere a statement may appear. The scope of a variable is from the point of its declaration until the end of the enclosing block.[3] Member iterates through the elements of a set and compares elem against each element until a match is found, or until all elements have been unsuccessfully considered.

AddElem adds an element to a set. If the element is already in the set then nothing happens. Otherwise, it is inserted, provided there is room in the array.

```
ErrCode Set::AddElem (int elem)        // add elem to the set
{
    for (int i = 0; i < card; ++i)
        if (elems[i] == elem) return noErr;
    if (card < maxCard) {
        elems[card++] = elem;  return noErr;
    } else
        return overflow;
} /* AddElem */
```

---

[3]   Despite its appearance, the scope of i is the block that immediately encloses the loop, that is, the entire body of the function.

RmvElem does the reverse of AddElem; it removes an element from a set, provided that element is indeed in the set.

```
void Set::RmvElem (int elem)              // remove elem from the set
{
    for (int i = 0; i < card; ++i)
        if (elems[i] == elem) {
            for (; i < card-1; ++i)       // shift elements left
                elems[i] = elems[i+1];
            --card;
        }
} /* RmvElem */
```

Copy copies one set to another. The parameter of this function is a pointer to the destination set. As the function shows, we can still refer to the private part of the class by dereferencing this pointer.

```
void Set::Copy (Set* set)                 // copy a set into another
{
    for (int i = 0; i < card; ++i)
        set->elems[i] = elems[i];
    set->card = card;
} /* Copy */
```

Equal compares two sets for equality. Two sets are equal if they contain exactly the same elements (remember that the order of the elements is immaterial). Note how Equal calls Member, checking if elems[i] is a member of set.

```
Bool Set::Equal (Set* set)                // test if two sets are equal
{
    if (card != set->card) return false;
    for (int i = 0; i < card; ++i)
        if (!set->Member(elems[i]))
            return false;
    return true;
} /* Equal */
```

Print prints the contents of a set using the conventional mathematical notation. For example, a set containing the numbers 5, 2, and 10 is printed as {5,2,10}.

```
void Set::Print ()                      // print a set as {...}
{
    cout << "{";
    for (int i = 0; i < card-1; ++i)
        cout << elems[i] << ",";
    if (card > 0)                       // no comma after the last element
        cout << elems[card-1];
    cout << "}\n";
} /* Print */
```

In Print, output is performed using statement of the form cout << expr, where cout is the default output stream of C++ (streams are described in Section 9.6). If we write Print using the old style of output in C, it will look like this:

```
void Set::Print ()                      // in old C style
{
    printf("{");
    for (int i = 0; i < card-1; ++i)
        printf("%1d,",elems[i]);
    if (card > 0)
        printf("%1d",elems[card-1]);
    printf("}\n");
} /* Print */
```

This is still valid C++ code, but the use of cout is arguably neater.

EXERCISE 1.1   *solution provided*
Introduce a new member for Set, named Card, which returns the cardinality of a set. Code Card as an inline function.

EXERCISE 1.2   *solution provided*
Code the function members Intersect and Union. Both should compare the elements of two sets s1 and s2 to produce a third set s3. Intersect should return in s3 all elements that are in both s1 and s2. Union should return in s3 all elements that are in either s1 or s2. For example, the intersection of {2,5,3} and {7,5,2} is {2,5} and their union is {2,5,3,7}.

EXERCISE 1.3   *solution provided*
Introduce two new members for Set, named Subset and PSubset. Subset should return true if all elements of a set s1 are in another set s2, and false otherwise. PSubset is the same as Subset, except that it should return false when s1 and s2 are equal.

The Set class can be tested using a simple driver. As in C, execution in C++ always starts from the main function. The following main function creates 3 sets and calls the various function members of `Set`.

```
main ()                          // a simple test for the Set class
{
    Set s1, s2, s3;
    s1.EmptySet ();   s2.EmptySet ();   s3.EmptySet ();
    s1.AddElem (10);  s1.AddElem (20);  s1.AddElem (30);  s1.AddElem (40);
    s2.AddElem (30);  s2.AddElem (50);  s2.AddElem (10);  s2.AddElem (60);
    cout << "s1 = ";                s1.Print ();
    cout << "s2 = ";                s2.Print ();
    s2.RmvElem (50);
    cout << "s2 - {50} = ";         s2.Print ();
    if (s1.Member (20))
        cout << "20 is in s1\n";
    s1.Intersect (&s2, &s3);
    cout << "s1 intsec s2 = ";      s3.Print ();
    s1.Union (&s2, &s3);
    cout << "s1 union s2 = ";       s3.Print ();
    if (!s1.Equal (&s2))
        cout << "s1 /= s2\n";
} /* main */
```

If we include the class `Set` and the `main` function in one file, the organization of the file should be as follows.

```
#include <stream.h>
const maxCard = 16;
enum Bool { false, true };
enum ErrCode { noErr, overflow };

class Set {
    ...
};

... function members ...

main ()
{
    ...
}
```

Other arrangements are also possible, so long as the `const` and `enum` declarations appear before the class. The first line in the file is an `include` directive and causes the contents of the header file `stream.h` to be textually included in that position.

You should include stream.h in every file that uses the I/O facilities of C++. This is similar to the use of the header file stdio.h in C.

1.5 Compilation

To compile C++ programs, follow the instruction supplied with your C++ compiler. The exact commands and steps may vary from one installation to another. The following examples are given as illustration.

The command for the UNIX-based AT&T C++ compiler is CC. Assuming that the program developed in the previous section is in a file named set.cc, the following two commands compile and run the program.[4]

```
$ CC set.cc
$ a.out
s1 = {10,20,30,40}
s2 = {30,50,10,60}
s2 - {50} = {30,10,60}
20 is in s1
s1 intsec s2 = {10,30}
s1 union s2 = {30,10,60,20,40}
s1 /= s2
$
```

where $ is the UNIX prompt and user input appears in **bold**. The first line causes set.cc to be compiled. In UNIX, the executable file produced by the compiler is placed in a file named a.out. Typing this name as a command runs the program, producing the output shown above.

The command for running the GNU C++ compiler available for SUN workstations is g++. The rest is as before.

```
$ g++ set.cc
$ a.out
...output as above...
$
```

Like C compilers, UNIX-based C++ compilers also allow the use of compiler options. For example, the -o option places the executable code in a user-specified file, and the -c option allows separate compilation of files.

---

[4]   In both AT&T and GNU C++, a source file should end in one of .c, .C, or .cc. We have used the .cc convention throughout this book.

EXERCISE 1.4

Type in the set.cc program and compile it. Once you have it running, break the code into 3 files, as suggested below.

```
set.h:    #include <stream.h>
          const and enum declarations
          the declaration of the Set class
set.cc:   #include "set.h"
          the definition of the function members
main.cc:  #include "set.h"
          the definition of main
```

Separately compile the files, place the executable code in a file named set, and run the program.

```
$ g++ -c set.cc main.cc
$ g++ set.o main.o -o set
$ set
...
```

1.6 Summary

An (abstract) **data type** consists of two things: a concrete representation of the objects of the type, and a set of private operations that characterize the type.

New data types are defined using the **class** construct. A class declaration may consist of two parts: a private part (accessible to the type operations only) and a public part which constitutes the class interface to the outside world. The operations of a type are defined as **function** members.

Function members (or in fact any function) can be declared to be **inline**. This is typically used to avoid the overhead of a function call for small and frequently used functions.

Constants and enumerations are defined, respectively, using the **const** and **enum** constructs. These are preferred over the use of macros.

When a function member is called, it receives an **implicit** argument which denotes the object for which the function was called.

A program which performs I/O should include the **stream.h** header file. Similarly, user-defined header files can be used to separate constant, enumeration, type, macro, and class declarations from function definitions.

CHAPTER 2

Constructors and Destructors

To enable user-defined data types to behave like the built-in data types, we need an implicit way of relating the lifetime of an object to its scope. We also need a way to initialize objects when defining them. Constructors and destructors support such features. This chapter describes the way constructors and destructors are defined for a class, and illustrates their application using a symbol table example. Specification of default arguments for functions and issues related to providing alternative implementations for the function members of a class are also discussed.

2.1 Constructors

Recall that in C, variables of a built-in type can be defined and initialized at once. C++ provides a means of defining and initializing objects of a class in a similar way. This is supported by special function members called **constructors**. A constructor is identified by the fact that it has the same name as the class itself. For example,

```
class Point {
    int xVal, yVal;
public:
        Point (int x, int y)    {xVal = x;  yVal = y;}    // constructor
    void OffsetPt (int, int);
};
```

is an alternative definition of the `Point` class (Section 1.2), where `SetPt` has been replaced by a constructor, which in turn is defined to be inline. Now we can define objects of type `Point` and initialize them at once. This is in fact *compulsory* for classes that contain constructors that require arguments.

```
Point pt1 = Point(10,20);
Point pt2;                          // illegal
```

The former can also be specified in an *abbreviated* form.

```
Point pt1(10,20);
```

A class may, in general, have more than one constructor, but these must be different in terms of the type or number of arguments they take so that the compiler can choose the appropriate one. For example,

```
class Point {
      int xVal, yVal;
public:
            Point (int x, int y)      { xVal = x;  yVal = y; }
            Point (float, float);    // polar coordinates
            Point ()                 { xVal = yVal = 0; }   // origin
      void OffsetPt (int, int);
};

Point::Point (float len, float angle)    // polar coordinates
{
      xVal = (int) (len * cos(angle));
      yVal = (int) (len * sin(angle));
}
```

offers 3 different constructors. An object of type `Point` can be defined using any of these.

```
Point pt1(10,20);                // cartesian coordinates
Point pt2(60.3,3.14);            // polar coordinates
Point pt3;                       // origin
```

The use of constructors ensures that proper initialization of objects will not be overlooked. For example, in the `Set` class (Section 1.4), if we define an object of type `Set` and forget to call `EmptySet` then `card` will be undefined for that object, and things can go seriously wrong. Use of a constructor eliminates the possibility of this ever happening.

```
class Set {
    int elems[maxCard];
    int card;
public:
    Set ()            { card = 0; }    // constructor
    // ...
};
```

A constructor requires no return type; the return type is implicit and is a pointer to the class itself.

2.2 Dynamic storage

Recall that in C, dynamic storage is allocated and reclaimed using library functions such as `malloc` and `free`. In addition to these, C++ offers two operators, `new` and `delete`, that can be used in a similar capacity. For example, the following two definitions of `str` are equivalent.

```
char* str = malloc(20);        // C style
char* str = new char[20];      // C++ style
```

In either case, `str` is set to point to a sequence of 20 chars allocated dynamically on the heap. The difference is that, whereas `malloc` is given the number of chars to be allocated, `new` accepts as its operand a proper type – in this case, an array of 20 chars. The operand can be anything, so long as it is a valid type.

```
struct Person { char* name, int age; };
Person* p = (Person*) malloc(sizeof(Person));    // C style
Person* p = new Person;                           // C++ style
```

In this case, `new` allocates a structure of type `Person` and returns a pointer to it. Unlike `malloc`, `new` requires no type casting. The type of a pointer returned by `new` is always `void*`. When `new` fails to allocate a block of the required size, it returns 0. By definition:

- A pointer of type `void*` is compatible with any pointer type.
- Zero (0) is a valid pointer, compatible with any pointer type. C++ guarantees that 0 is a unique pointer, that is, no object is ever allocated at address 0.

These two rules imply that working with pointers in C++ involves much less type casting than in C. The compiler does most of the work.

To reclaim a block allocated by `new`, we can call `delete`; this is also a unary operator.

```
free (str);                    // C style
delete str;                    // C++ style
```

Applying `delete` to a pointer with value 0 is harmless.

2.3 Example: a symbol table

A symbol table is a collection of symbols and their attributes. To further illustrate the use of constructors, in this section we develop a symbol table as a class. For simplicity we assume that a symbol (represented as a string) has only one attribute (an integer value).

A popular way of implementing symbol tables is to use a hash and link technique. The symbol table consists of *n* slots (0 through *n*-1). A hash function is applied to each symbol to decide in which slot it should be stored. Symbols having the same hash address are stored in the same slot and arranged as a linked-list.

We represent each symbol using a structure, containing its name, its value, and a pointer to the next symbol.

```
typedef int SymValue;
struct Symbol {
    char*    name;             // symbol name
    SymValue value;            // symbol value
    Symbol*  next;             // pointer to next symbol in the list
};
```

The symbol table itself is defined as a class.

```
class SymTable {
    Symbol** table;            // table of slots
    int      size;             // no. of slots
    int Hash (char*);          // the hash function
public:
             SymTable (int);   // constructor
    Symbol* AddSym (char*, SymValue);
    Symbol* FindSym (char*);
    Bool     RmvSym (char*);
    void     PrintTable ();
};
```

Note that instead of defining `table` as a fixed-size array of `Symbol` pointers, we have defined it as a double pointer. In this way, we can create symbol tables of different sizes. The desired size of a table is passed as an argument to the constructor, which in turn allocates storage for it.

```
SymTable::SymTable (int sz)      // constructor
{
     if (sz <= 0) {               // bad size
         size = 0;
         table = 0;
     } else if ((table = new Symbol*[size = sz]) != 0)
         for (int i = 0; i < size; ++i)
             table[i] = 0;        // all slots initially empty
     else
         size = 0;
} /* SymTable */
```

The constructor also checks for errors: if the requested size is invalid or if `new` fails, both `size` and `table` are set to 0.

The `Hash` function is included in the private part of the class, because it is only used by the function members. `Hash` adds up the codes of the characters in a name and returns the remainder of dividing the sum by `size`. This ensures that a hash address is always in the range `0..size-1`.

```
int SymTable::Hash (char* name) // the hash function
{
     int slot = 0;
     while (*name)
         slot += *name++;
     return slot % size;
} /* Hash */
```

`AddSym` creates a new entry for a symbol, provided it can allocate storage for it. It uses `Hash` to decide in which slot the symbol should be placed and then inserts the entry in front of the linked-list denoted by that slot.

```
Symbol* SymTable::AddSym (char* name,SymValue value)   // add a symbol
{
     Symbol* sym;
     int slot = Hash(name);
     if ((sym = new Symbol) != 0 &&
         (sym->name = new char[strlen(name)+1]) != 0) {
```

```
            strcpy(sym->name, name);
            sym->value = value;
            sym->next = table[slot];
            table[slot] = sym;
            return sym;
        } else {                            // new failed
            delete sym;
            sym = 0;
        }
        return sym;         ←— Just one exit please!
    } /* AddSym */
```

AddSym returns a 0 pointer when it fails to allocate storage for a symbol. This enables the caller of AddSym to find out whether the request has been successful.

FindSym searches the symbol table for a symbol and returns a pointer to its entry if it finds it. Otherwise, it returns a 0 pointer.

```
Symbol* SymTable::FindSym (char* name)
{
    int slot = Hash(name);
    for (Symbol* sym = table[slot]; sym; sym = sym->next)
        if (strcmp(sym->name, name) == 0)
            break;
    return sym;
} /* FindSym */
```

The example is incorrect!

EXERCISE 2.1   *solution provided*

Code the RmvSym function member. It should search the table for a given symbol and remove its entry from the table, freeing the storage it occupies. RmvSym should return true when it finds and removes a symbol entry successfully, and false otherwise.

PrintTable is used for testing purposes. It prints the symbols in the table together with their associated values. Note the use of form in this function; it allows formatted output much in the same way printf is used in C.

Use SetW Param manipulators

```
void SymTable::PrintTable ()     // print the symbols and values
{
    for (int i = 0; i < size; ++i)
        for (Symbol* sym = table[i]; sym; sym = sym->next)
            cout << form("%20s %10d\n", sym->name, sym->value);
} /* PrintTable */
```

The SymTable class can be tested with the following driver. The declaration inside the function defines a variable, tab, of type SymTable. This causes the constructor for the class to be called implicitly with the value 16 as argument.

```
main ()                          // a simple driver to test SymTable class
{
    // construct a table of 16 slots:
    SymTable tab(16);
    // random words and page numbers from a book:
    tab.AddSym("whenever",109);   tab.AddSym("interface",142);
    tab.AddSym("finally",210);    tab.AddSym("providing",236);
    tab.AddSym("block",249);      tab.AddSym("comparison",128);
    tab.AddSym("alternative",64);
    tab.PrintTable();
    cout << "block has value: "
         << tab.FindSym("block")->value << "\n"
         << "interface has value: "
         << tab.FindSym("interface")->value << "\n";
    tab.RmvSym("finally");
    tab.RmvSym("interface");
    tab.PrintTable();
} /* main */
```

Compiling and running this program will produce the following output:

```
                interface       142
                providing       236
                 whenever       109
               comparison       128
                    block       249
              alternative        64
                  finally       210
block has value: 249
interface has value: 142
                providing       236
                 whenever       109
               comparison       128
                    block       249
              alternative        64
```

EXERCISE 2.2   *Get*   *solution provided*

Define two extra function members, SetValue and SymValue, for the SymTable class. SetValue sets the value of a symbol to a new value. If the symbol is not already in the table then SetValue should create an entry for it. GetValue returns the value of a symbol in a parameter. Both functions should return true when successful and false otherwise.

```
class SymTable {
    //...
public:
    //...
    Bool SetValue (char* name, SymValue val);
    Bool GetValue (char* name, SymValue* val);
};
```

2.4 Default arguments

It is sometimes convenient to specify default argument values for a function; these are used when the caller chooses not to specify the value of an argument. The constructor for SymTable above, for example, is a suitable candidate for this technique. A default value for a function argument is specified in the function declaration.

```
class SymTable {
    //...
public:
    SymTable (int sz = 16);     // constructor with default arg value
    //...
};
```

The actual definition of the function remains unchanged. However, we now have the choice of either specifying a size for the table when we define a variable of type SymTable, or leaving it unspecified (i.e., use the default value).

```
SymTable tab1;          // table of 16 slots
SymTable tab2(16);      // table of 16 slots
SymTable tab3(64);      // table of 64 slots
```

Use of default arguments is not confined to function members; they can be used in global function as well. A default argument value can be specified either in a function declaration or in its implementation. The former convention is generally preferred. All default arguments must be trailing arguments.

```
Point(int x = 0, int y = 0);    // correct
Point(int, int y = 0);          // correct
Point(int x = 0, int);          // wrong
```

A default argument need not necessarily be a constant. Arbitrary expressions can be used, so long as the variables used in the expression are available to the scope of the function definition.

2.5 Destructors

The symbol table example above does not include any means of deallocating a table. This can be provided as a function member which goes through the table slots, deletes all the entries, and finally the table itself. The disadvantage of this approach is that there is no guarantee that the programmer will not forget to call the function.

This difficulty is overcome by a special kind of function member called a **destructor**. Just as a constructor initializes an object when it is declared, a destructor destroys the object when its name goes out of scope. A destructor has always the same name as the class, but is preceded by a ~ symbol.

```
class SymTable {
    //...
public:
    SymTable (int sz = 16);    // constructor
    ~SymTable ();              // destructor
    //...
};

SymTable::~SymTable ()             // destructor
{
    for (int i = 0; i < size; ++i)
        for (Symbol *sym = table[i], *tmp; sym; ) {
            sym = (tmp = sym)->next;
            delete tmp->name;
            delete tmp;
        }
    if (size > 0)
        delete table;
} /* ~SymTable */
```

Now consider what happens when a symbol table is declared and used in a function.

```
void Foo()
{
    SymTable tab(32);
    //...
}
```

When `Foo` is called, the constructor for `tab` is called first, allocating storage for and initializing the symbol table. Next the body of `Foo` is executed. Finally, before `Foo` returns, the destructor for `tab` is called last, deleting the storage occupied by it. Hence, as far as storage allocation is concerned, `tab` behaves just like automatic variables, which are created when the enclosing function is called and die when the function returns.

Such consistency of behaviour is extremely useful and important. Without it, the user of a class that uses dynamic storage has the extra responsibility of ensuring that objects are initialized and freed in the right order. The implicit nature of constructors and destructors eliminates this unnecessary burden.

EXERCISE 2.3   *solution provided*

Define a binary sorted tree class named `BinTree`. Each node in the tree should have an integer key and the tree should be sorted in ascending key order. Define the following function members for `BinTree`:

- A constructor which initializes a tree to be empty.
- A destructor.
- `Insert` which inserts a new key into a tree.
- `Delete` which deletes a key from a tree.
- `Print` which prints the keys in a tree in ascending order.

2.6 Alternative implementations

It is often useful to view the implementation of the function members of a class as separate from the class itself. The latter is called the **specification** of a class; its public part contains all the information that a programmer will require in order to use the class. The **implementation** of a class is embodied by the internal details of function members.

Good classes are designed so that some degree of implementation flexibility is maintained. That is, so far as possible, one should be able to change the implementation of a class (to, for example, introduce a different algorithm) without changing the specification of the class. The obvious advantage of this is the ability to provide alternative implementations for the same class without requiring the programs that use the class to be changed.

When considering alternative implementations for a class, three types of change are possible:

[1] The internal details of the function members have to be changed, but everything else remains unchanged. This is the most desirable case, but not always possible.

[2] The data members of the class need to be modified as well. For example, new data may have to be introduced, or the type of existing data needs to be changed.

[3] The function members of the class need to be modified as well. For example, new function members may have to be introduced, or the specification of the arguments of existing functions needs to be changed.

Changes of type [2] are undesirable, since they generally require additional changes to programs that use the class. Changes of type [3] are most undesirable, since their impact on the programs that use the class can be quite substantial.

The time spent in considering these issues when designing a new class is an investment that is well rewarded in the future. Insight to the design of a class is gained by carefully considering all potential alternatives, and choosing the one which minimizes future change effort.

Providing alternative implementations for the same class also requires some forethought to be paid to the way the text of the class is arranged. In particular, the specification of a class should be separated from its implementation, that is, they should appear in separate files. For example, a class, Sample, which has two alternative implementations should be arranged as at least 3 files.

```
Sample.h:      class Sample {
                   //...
               };

Sample1.cc:    #include "Sample.h"
               // first implementation of function members
               // ...

Sample2.cc:    #include "Sample.h"
               // second implementation of function members
               // ...
```

EXERCISE 2.4   *solution provided*

Break down the code for SymTable into 2 files, as suggested above. Attempt an alternative implementation of the class by redefining the function members AddSym and RmvSym so that they keep the entries in each linked-list alphabetically sorted at all times. Redefine FindSym so that it takes advantage of this to avoid the searching of an entire list when the search item is not in the list.

2.7 Summary

A **constructor** is a member of a class that has the same name as the class and defines the way each object of the class is created and initialized. Each time an object of a class is defined, its constructor is applied to it implicitly.

A **destructor** is a member of a class that has the same name as the class, preceded by a ~ symbol. A destructor does the reverse of a constructor: it frees the storage occupied by an object. When an object name goes out of scope its destructor is applied to it implicitly.

In C++, dynamic storage allocations and reclamation are supported by the **new** and **delete** operators. Unlike malloc, new takes a type as its operand. It returns a pointer of type void* which is compatible with any pointer type. New returns 0 when it fails. Applying delete to a 0 pointer is harmless.

A function (member or global) can have **default argument** values. When a function is called, the caller can leave such arguments unspecified, in which case the default value is assumed. C++ requires all default arguments to be trailing arguments.

When designing a class, one should consider all potential **design alternatives** and choose the one which lends itself best to change. A good class definition ensures that most future changes will only affect the implementation of function members and not the specification of the class.

The **specification** and **implementation** of a class should appear in separate files. This simplifies the task of providing alternative implementations for the class.

Friends

Occasionally we need to grant a function access to the private parts of two or more classes, so that it can be implemented efficiently. This chapter shows how this is facilitated by declaring the function to be a friend of such classes. Use of friends is illustrated by an example which involves conversion between sequences and binary trees.

3.1 Friend functions

Recall the set class (Section 1.4) and suppose that we have defined two variants of this class, one for sets of integers and one for sets of reals.

```
class IntSet {
      int elems[maxCard];
      int card;
public:  //...
};

class RealSet {
      float elems[maxCard];
      int    card;
public:  //...
};
```

We want to define a function, SetToReal, which converts an integer set to a real set. We can do this by making the function a member of IntSet.

```
void IntSet::SetToReal (RealSet* set)
{
    set->EmptySet();
    for (int i = 0; i < card; ++i)
        set->AddElem((float) elems[i]);
}
```

This will work, but the overhead of calling AddElem for every member of the set is unnecessary. The implementation can be improved if we could gain access to the private part of *both* IntSet and RealSet, but being only a member of IntSet, this is not possible.

C++ has a simple solution for such cases: a nonmember function can gain access to the private part of a class by declaring it to be a friend of the class. SetToReal, for example, can be declared to be a friend of both InSet and RealSet.

```
class IntSet {
    //...
public:
    friend void SetToReal (IntSet*,RealSet*);
    //...
};

class RealSet {
    //...
public:
    friend void SetToReal (IntSet*,RealSet*);
    //...
};
```

Although a friend declaration appears inside a class, that does *not* make the function a member of the class. When the function is called, it does not receive an implicit argument (as function members do). So, in essence, a friend function is like any other nonmember function and obeys the same scope rules. The one and only difference is that it has access to the private parts of the classes inside which it appears.

Having declared SetToReal a friend of both classes, we can now implement it more efficiently.

```
void SetToReal (IntSet* iSet,RealSet* rSet)
{
     rSet->card = iSet->card;
     for (int i = 0; i < iSet->card; ++i)
         rSet->elems[i] = (float) iSet->elems[i];
}
```

In general, the position of a friend declaration in a class is irrelevant: whether it appears in the private part or the public part, it has the same meaning. Putting such declarations in the public part, however, makes the code more readable.

3.2 Friend members

It is possible for a function member of one class to be a friend of another class. For example, SetToReal can be a member of IntSet and a friend of RealSet. Similarly, SetToInt, a function which converts a real set into an integer set, can be a member of RealSet and a friend of IntSet.

```
class RealSet;                      // this is necessary

class IntSet {
     //...
public:
     void SetToReal (RealSet*);
     friend void RealSet::SetToInt (IntSet*);
     //...
};

class RealSet {
     //...
public:
     void SetToInt (IntSet*);
     friend void IntSet::SetToReal (RealSet*);
     //...
};
```

The first line above declares RealSet as a class. This is necessary because IntSet refers to RealSet before the declaration of the latter. We can now define SetToReal and SetToInt as proper function members of a single argument.

```
void IntSet::SetToReal (RealSet* set)
{
    set->card = card;
    for (int i = 0; i < card; ++i)
        set->elems[i] = (float) elems[i];
}

void RealSet::SetToInt (IntSet* set)
{
    set->card = card;
    for (int i = 0; i < card; ++i)
        set->elems[i] = (int) elems[i];
}
```

The extreme case of having all function members of a class A as friends of another class B can be expressed in an *abbreviated* form.

```
class A;
class B {
    friend class A;              // abbreviated form
    //...
};
```

3.3 Example: sequence and binary tree

Consider two class definitions for sequences and binary trees, and assume that we want to define a constructor for `BinaryTree`, which converts a sequence into a 'balanced' tree.

```
class Sequence {                 // sequence of sorted items
    int* items;
    int  size, used;
public:
    //...
};

struct Node {                    // node in a binary tree
    int    item;
    Node* left;
    Node* right;
};
```

```
class BinaryTree {                          // binary sorted tree
    Node* root;
public:
    BinaryTree ()                   { root = 0; }
    BinaryTree (Sequence*,int,int);     // sequence to binary tree
    //...
};
```

An efficient algorithm for this function (assuming that it has direct access to the private part of Sequence) is as follows. Take the mid-item of the sequence and make it the root of the tree. Generate the left and right subtrees by applying the same procedure (recursively) to the subsequences to the left and right of the mid-item. Repeat this until the final subsequences are either empty or contain only one item. This is not only efficient, it also ensures that the generated tree is almost balanced. Figure 3.1 illustrates the conversion.

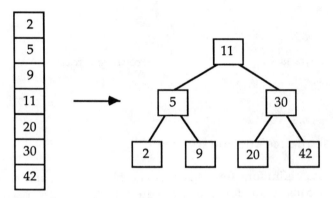

Figure 3.1 Conversion from a sequence to a binary tree.

The BinaryTree constructor takes three arguments: a sequence pointer, and two indices. The indices indicate the subsequence that is to be converted. The conversion is performed by an auxiliary function called MakeTree.

```
BinaryTree::BinaryTree (Sequence* seq,int low,int high)
{
    root = (low > high || low < 0 || high > seq->used)
            ? 0
            : MakeTree(seq,low,high);
} /* BinaryTree */
```

```
Node* MakeTree (Sequence* seq, int low, int high)
{
    int mid = (low + high) / 2;
    Node* node = new Node;
    if (node != 0) {
        node->item = seq->items[mid];
        node->left = (mid <= low ? 0 : MakeTree(seq, low, mid-1));
        node->right = (mid >= high ? 0 : MakeTree(seq, mid+1, high));
    }
    return node;
} /* MakeTree */
```

Both the constructor `BinaryTree` and the auxiliary function `MakeTree` refer to the private part of `Sequence`, and hence should be declared as friends of `Sequence`.

```
class BinaryTree;
class Sequence {
    int* items;
    int  size, used;
public:
    //...
    friend BinaryTree* BinaryTree::BinaryTree (Sequence*, int, int);
    friend Node*       MakeTree (Sequence*, int, int);
};
```

Note the way the return value of the first friend is declared as `BinaryTree*`, whereas the declaration of this function (as a member) in the `BinaryTree` class requires no indication of the return value. This is because the latter is a constructor declaration and the return type is implicit in the declaration; the return type of a constructor is always a pointer to the class. Of course, one can make this explicit.

```
class BinaryTree {
    Node* root;
public:
    BinaryTree* BinaryTree (Sequence*, int, int);
    //...
};
```

This is however unnecessary and in most implementations produces a warning message.

EXERCISE 3.1   *solution provided*

Use the technique illustrated by the above example to define another constructor for
`Sequence`, which converts a binary tree (supplied as an argument) to a sorted sequence.
Assume that there is a member in `BinaryTree` which returns the size (i.e., the number of
nodes) of a tree.

```
class Sequence {
    //...
public:
    //...
    Sequence (BinaryTree*);
    friend void MakeSeq (Node*,Sequence*);
};

class BinaryTree {
    //...
public:
    //...
    int TreeSize ();
    friend Sequence* Sequence::Sequence (BinaryTree*);
};
```

3.4 Default arguments revisited

`BinaryTree` would be easier to use if it had default argument values for `low` and
`high`, so that, for example,

```
Sequence s;
//...
BinaryTree b(&s);
```

would convert the entire sequence `s` into a binary tree `b`. To do this, one might be
tempted to write:

```
BinaryTree::BinaryTree (Sequence* seq,
                        int low = 0,int high = seq->used)    // wrong
{   //...
}
```

This is plainly wrong, because the default value `seq->used` is undefined: `seq` is a
parameter to the function; it can take part in an expression in the body of the
function, but not in the function header.

A reasonable solution in this case is to specify the default value of both `low` and `high` as 0 and then check the value of `high` inside the function.

```
BinaryTree::BinaryTree (Sequence* seq, int low = 0, int high = 0)
{
    if (high == 0)
        high = seq->used;
    root = (low > high || low < 0 || high > seq->used)
           ? 0 : MakeTree(seq, low, high);
} /* BinaryTree */
```

EXERCISE 3.2   *solution provided*

Modify the constructor for `BinaryTree` and the auxiliary function `MakeTree` so that, when `low` is greater than `high`, the tree is generated in reverse order (i.e., decreasing order of items).

3.5 Implicit member argument

As noted earlier (Section 1.2), when a function member of a class is called it receives an implicit argument which denotes the particular object (of the class) for which the function was called. For example, in

```
Point pt (10,20);
pt.OffsetPt (2,2);
```

`pt` is an implicit argument to `OffsetPt`. Within the body of a function member, one can refer to this argument explicitly as `this`, which denotes a pointer to the object for which the member was invoked. Using `this`, `OffsetPt` can be rewritten as:

```
Point::OffsetPt (int x, int y)
{
    this->xVal += x;        // equivalent to: xVal += x;
    this->yVal += y;        // equivalent to: yVal += y;
}
```

Whether you use `this` or not, the code generated by the compiler is the same (the `this` version, in fact, betrays the way the compiler works).

You must, however, bear in mind that `this` is defined for function members *only*. In particular, it is undefined for a friend function (unless the function is also a member of some class).

EXERCISE 3.3   *solution provided*
      Rewrite Union (see Exercise 1.2) using the explicit this argument. Which version is more
      readable? Why?

3.6 Name resolution

When calling a function member, we usually use an abbreviated form. For
example, the two calls

```
pt.OffsetPt(2,2);              // abbreviated form
pt.Point::OffsetPt(2,2);       // full form
```

are equivalent. The compiler always substitutes the latter for the former. This
reflects the fact that the members of a class are *local* to the class. Hence, one can
define two or more classes that have members with identical names, without
causing any ambiguity. For example, suppose both IntSet and RealSet (Section
3.1) have a member called Print, which prints the elements of a set. There must
be two implementations of Print, one for IntSet and one for RealSet.

```
void IntSet::Print ()
{    //...
}

void RealSet::Print ()
{    //...
}
```

Now, one can define objects of either type and call Print as usual.

```
IntSet is;
RealSet rs;

//...
is.Print();                    // i.e., is.IntSet::Print();
rs.Print();                    // i.e., rs.RealSet::Print();
```

By examining the type of the object (is or rs), the compiler can determine which
Print should be used.
     A function f can be a member and a friend of a class A at the same time, in
which case there is more than one definition for f, all of which are distinct.

```
class A {
    //...
public:
    void f ();                    // void A::f()
    friend int B::f (int);        // int B::f(int)
    friend int f (char*);         // int f(char*)
};
```

Here, there are 3 distinct definitions of f; the first one is local to A, the second one is local to B, and the third one is global.

When a name is defined in two nested scopes, one can override the normal scope rules, using the name resolution operator ::. For example, in

```
class Point {
    int x, y;
public:
    Point (int x, int y)          { Point::x = x; Point::y = y; }
    //...
}
```

x and y in the constructor (inner scope) hide x and y in the class (outer scope). The latter are referred to explicitly as Point::x and Point::y.

The resolution operator is both unary and binary. When used as a unary operator, it refers to the definition of a name in the outermost scope (i.e., its global definition).

```
int x = 0;                        // global
void Foo (char* x)
{
    int y = ::x;                  // global x
    //...
}
```

This rule applies, regardless of whether the operand of :: is a variable or a function name. The latter is useful for calling system routines within a function member that has the same name.

```
Class Process {
    //...
public:
    int fork ();
    //...
};
```

```
int Process::fork ()
{
    int pid = ::fork();          // use system fork
    //...
}
```

Applying :: to a nonglobal name leads to a compilation error.

3.7 Summary

A function can be granted access to the private part of one or more classes by declaring it to be a **friend** of such classes. A class can have a friend and a member that have the same name; these, however, denote two separate functions. A function can be a member of a class and a friend of another class.

Use of **default argument** values for constructors often simplifies their use.

The implicit argument of a function member can be explicitly referred to as this. The type of this is a pointer to the class. This is not defined for a friend function which is not a member of any class.

The **name resolution** operator :: is used to explicitly indicate a variable by its scope. When used as a binary operator, its left operand should be a class name and its right operand should be a class member. When used as a unary operator, its operand should be a global name.

Overloading

This chapter describes how function and operator names can be overloaded by creating additional definitions for them. The use of the overload facility is illustrated by redefining the Set class developed in Chapter 1. Built-in and user-defined type conversion rules are discussed and exemplified by a class for representing binary numbers. Finally, an example of overloading subscript and call operators is given.

4.1 Function overloading

Consider a function, GetTime, which returns in its parameter(s) the current time, and suppose that we require two variants of this function: one which returns the time as seconds from midnight, and one which returns the time as hours, minutes, and seconds. There is no reason for these two function variants to have different names, after all they do the same thing.

C++ allows functions to be **overloaded**, that is, the same function to have more than one definition.

```
overload GetTime;
void GetTime (long* ticks);          // seconds from midnight
void GetTime (int* hours,int* minutes,int* seconds);
```

The first line instructs the compiler that GetTime is overloaded (i.e., has multiple definitions) and should appear before all declarations/definitions of GetTime.

When `GetTime` is called, the compiler compares the number and type of arguments in the call against the definitions of `GetTime` and chooses the one that matches the call. For this reason, all definitions of an overloaded function should differ in their number or type of parameters.

Overload declarations are only necessary for functions that have multiple *global* definitions (e.g., `GetTime` above). If a function `f` has different definitions in different scopes (e.g., `f` is a member of classes A, B, and C, and also has a global definition) then there is no need to declare `f` as overloaded; the compiler picks the correct definition by examining the context of a call. Also, in this case, the definitions of `f` need not differ in any way.

All function members of a class are overloaded by default, requiring no `overload` declaration.

```
class Time {
    //...
    void GetTime (long* ticks);
    void GetTime (int* hours,int* minutes,int* seconds);
};
```

Function overloading is useful for obtaining flavors that are not possible using default arguments alone. Overloaded functions may also have default arguments.

```
overload Error;
void Error (int errCode,char* errMsg = "");
void Error (char* errMsg);
```

EXERCISE 4.1   *solution provided*
> Write overloaded versions of a `Max` function which compares two integers, or reals, or strings and returns the 'larger' one.

4.2 Operator overloading

All operators in C++ are by definition overloaded. For example, consider how the following uses of the division operator differ in their types of operands and result:

```
55.62 / 2.22        ⟹ 25.05405405
105 / 20            ⟹ 5
105 / 20.0          ⟹ 5.25
```

C++ offers a facility for defining additional meanings for such operators. For example, we can further overload the + and – operators for adding and subtracting points.[1]

```
class Point {
      int x, y;
public:
      Point (int x, int y);         { Point::x = x; Point::y = y; }
      Point operator + (Point p)  { return Point (x + p.x, y + p.y); }
      Point operator - (Point p)  { return Point (x - p.x, y - p.y); }
};
```

After this definition, + and – can be used for adding and subtracting points, much as they are used for adding and subtracting numbers.

```
Point p1 (10,20), p2 (10,20);
Point p3 = p1 + p2;
Point p4 = p1 - p2;
```

Since + and – are binary operators, one can improve the readability of their definition by declaring them as friends rather than members of Point.

```
class Point {
      int x, y;
public:
      //...
      friend Point operator + (Point p, Point q)
                                { return Point (p.x + q.x, p.y + q.y); }
      friend Point operator - (Point p, Point q)
                                { return Point (p.x - q.x, p.y - q.y); }
};
```

In general, to overload a predefined operator ∂, we define a function named operator∂. If ∂ is a **binary** operator:

- operator∂ must take exactly one argument if defined as a class member, or two arguments if defined as a friend or globally.

However, if ∂ is a **unary** operator:

- operator∂ must take no arguments if defined as a function member, or one argument if defined as a friend or globally.

---

[1]   Operators can also be overloaded globally.

The following predefined operators can be overloaded:[2]

unary:	+	−	*	!	~	&	++	−−	()	−>	new delete

binary:	+	−	*	/	%	&	|	^	<<	>>
	=	+=	−=	/=	%=	&=	|=	^=	<<=	>>=
	==	!=	<	>	<=	>=	&&	||	[]	()

A strictly unary operator (e.g., ~) cannot be defined as binary, nor can a strictly binary operator (e.g., =) be defined as unary.

C++ does not support the definition of new operator tokens, because this can lead to ambiguity. Furthermore, the precedence rules for the predefined operators is fixed and cannot be altered. For example, no matter how you overload *, it always has a higher precedence than +.

Overloaded forms of ++ and −− can be used either as prefix or postfix, but the compiler will not distinguish between the prefix and postfix applications. Equivalence rules do not hold for overloaded operators. For example, overloading + does not affect +=, unless the latter is also explicitly overloaded. Operators (), [] and −> should always be overloaded as members and not friends.

4.3 Example: set operators

Recall the Set class (Section 1.4). Since set is a mathematical concept, defining set operations as operators can significantly improve the readability of set manipulating programs.

```
class Set {
        int elems[maxCard];
        int card;
public:
        Set ()                          { card = 0; }
        friend Bool operator &   (int,Set);      // membership
        friend Bool operator ==  (Set,Set);
        friend Bool operator !=  (Set,Set);
        friend Set  operator *   (Set,Set);      // intersection
        friend Set  operator +   (Set,Set);      // union
        friend Bool operator <   (Set,Set);      // proper subset
        friend Bool operator <=  (Set,Set);      // subset
        //...
};
```

---

2   The built-in type operators (e.g., int) can also be overloaded; see Section 4.4.

The definition of these functions is straightforward and similar to the original function members.[3]

```
Bool operator & (int elem,Set set)
{
        for (int i = 0; i < set.card; ++i)
            if (set.elems[i] == elem) return true;
        return false;
} /* operator & */

Bool operator == (Set set1,Set set2)
{
        if (set1.card != set2.card) return false;
        for (int i = 0; i < set1.card; ++i)
            if (!(set1.elems[i] & set2)) return false;
        return true;
} /* operator == */

inline Bool operator != (Set set1,Set set2)
{
        return !(set1 == set2);
} /* operator != */

Set operator * (Set set1,Set set2)
{
        Set res;
        for (int i = 0; i < set1.card; ++i)
            for (int j = 0; j < set2.card; ++j)
                if (set1.elems[i] == set2.elems[j]) {
                    res.elems[res.card++] = set1.elems[i];
                    break;
                }
        return res;
} /* operator * */
```

An overloaded operator can be applied using its conventional syntax, or by calling the function that implements it.

```
operator& (elem, set)          // explicit call
elem & set                     // abbreviated form
```

[3] Unlike Set, for some classes overloading == and != is redundant, since bitwise equality and inequality can be used instead (e.g., the Point class). Use of == and != for comparing objects of a user-defined type is always interpreted as bitwise unless they have been overloaded for that type.

The code generated by the compiler in either case is the same.

Unlike the earlier definition of Set, we did not pass a set as a pointer to the functions. The reason for this is that the operands of an overloaded operator cannot be *all* pointers.[4] The extra overhead of a set being copied each time it is passed to an operator can be overcome by the use of references (Section 5.2).

EXERCISE 4.2   *solution provided*
> Implement the + , <, and <= operators for the Set class. Note that < is easily defined in terms of <=.

4.4 Type conversion

The normal built-in type conversion rules of the language also apply to overloaded functions and operators. For example, in

```
if ('a' & set)
    //...
```

the first operand of & (i.e., 'a') is implicitly converted from char to int.

Any other type conversion required in addition to these must be explicitly defined by the programmer. For example, suppose we want to overload + for the Point type so that it can be used to add two points, or to add an integer value to both coordinates of a point.

```
class Point {
     int x, y;
public:
     //...
     friend Point operator + (Point,Point);
     friend Point operator + (int,Point);
     friend Point operator + (Point,int);
};
```

To make + commutative, we have defined two functions for adding an integer to a point; one for when the integer is the first operand, and one for when the integer is the second operand.

In general, it is easier to use a constructor to get a similar effect. In this case, we need a constructor which takes an integer, specifying both coordinates of a point.

---

4   Some operators are exempted from this rule. For example, unary * can be overloaded to return the 'contents of' a pointer in a user-defined manner. See Section 8.4 for an example.

```
class Point {
    int x, y;
public:
    //...
    Point (int x)              { Point::x = Point::y = x; }
    friend Point operator + (Point,Point);
};
```

For constructors of one argument, one need not explicitly call the constructor.

```
Point p = 10;                           // equivalent to: Point p(10);
```

Hence, it is possible to write expressions that involve variables or constants of type Point and int using the + operator.

```
Point p(10,20), q = 0;
q = p + 5;                              // equivalent to: q = p + Point(5);
```

Here, 5 is first converted to a temporary Point object and then added to p. The temporary object is then destroyed. The overall effect is an *implicit* type conversion from int to Point. The final value of q is therefore (15,25).

What if we want to do the opposite conversion, from a user-defined type to a built-in type? In this case, constructors cannot be used because they always return an object of the user-defined type. Instead, one can define a function member which explicitly converts the type. For example, to convert an object in class A to int we define a function member which does just that.

```
class A {
    //...
public:
    //...
    operator int ();            // convert from A to int
};
```

Recall how built-in types can be used as operators for type conversion (also called casting). Here, we have simply overloaded the int operator so that it can accept an object of type A as argument and properly convert it. The example in the next section illustrates a typical application of this technique.

4.5 Example: binary numbers

Consider the following class, which represents a 16-bit binary number as a sequence of 0 and 1 characters.

```
class Binary {
      char bits[16];                        // 16-bit quantity
public:
      Binary (char*);
      Binary (int);
      friend Binary operator + (Binary,Binary);
      operator int ();                      // type conversion
      void   Print ();
};
```

Two constructors are specified, one which produces a binary number from its bit pattern, and one which converts a positive integer to its equivalent binary representation.

```
Binary::Binary (char* num)
{
      int iSrc = strlen(num) - 1;
      int iDest = 15;

      while (iSrc >= 0 && iDest >= 0)   // copy bits
            bits[iDest--] = (num[iSrc--] == '0' ? '0' : '1');
      while (iDest >= 0)                // pad left with zeros
            bits[iDest--] = '0';
} /* Binary */

Binary::Binary (int num)
{
      for (int i = 15; i >= 0; --i) {
            bits[i] = (num % 2 == 0 ? '0' : '1');
            num >>= 1;
      }
} /* Binary */
```

The + operator is overloaded for adding two binary numbers. Addition is done bit by bit. For simplicity, no attempt is made to detect overflow.

```
Binary operator + (Binary n1, Binary n2)
{
    unsigned carry = 0;
    unsigned value;
    Binary res = "0";

    for (int i = 15; i >= 0; --i) {
        value = (n1.bits[i] == '0' ? 0 : 1) +
                (n2.bits[i] == '0' ? 0 : 1) + carry;
        res.bits[i] = (value % 2 == 0 ? '0' : '1');
        carry = value >> 1;
    }
    return res;
} /* operator + */
```

A type conversion operator is also defined and converts an object of type Binary to an int.

```
Binary::operator int ()
{
    unsigned value = 0;

    for (int i = 0; i <= 15; ++i)
        value = (value << 1) + (bits[i] == '0' ? 0 : 1);
    return value;
} /* operator int */
```

To facilitate quick testing of the program, a Print member is defined which simply prints the bit pattern of a binary number.

```
void Binary::Print ()
{
    char str[17];
    strncpy(str, bits, 16);
    str[16] = '\0';
    cout << str << "\n";
} /* Print */
```

The following driver creates two objects of type Binary and tests the + operator.

```
main ()
{
    Binary n1 = "1011";        // binary number
    Binary n2 = n1 + 15;       // add binary and decimal

    n1.Print();
    n2.Print();
    cout << n2 + 5 << "\n";     // add and then convert to int
    cout << n2 - 5 << "\n";     // convert n2 to int and then subtract
}
```

In the second line of main, the application of the + operator (n1 + 15) causes 15 to be converted to Binary before addition is performed. In an expanded form, it would look like:

```
Binary n2 = Binary::operator+(n1,Binary(15));
```

The last two lines of main are more interesting. The first of these two converts 5 to Binary, does the addition and then converts the Binary result to int, before sending it to cout. This is equivalent to:

```
cout << (int) Binary::operator+(n2,Binary(5)) << "\n";
```

The last line of main first converts n2 to int (because - is not defined for Binary), performs the subtraction and then send the result to cout. This is equivalent to:

```
cout << ((int) n2) - 5 << "\n";
```

In either case, the user-defined type conversion operator is applied implicitly. The output produced by the program is evidence that the conversions are performed correctly.

```
0000000000001011
0000000000011010
31
21
```

EXERCISE 4.3   *solution provided*
    Define operator- for the Binary class. For simplicity, assume that the first operand is always greater than the second operand.

4.6 Subscript and call operators

The subscript operator [] and the function call operator () can be overloaded in exactly the same manner as other operators. The former is always binary; the latter may be defined as unary or binary.

Recall the SymTable class (Section 2.3). We can overload the subscript and/or the call operator so that they can be used for finding the value of a symbol.

```
class SymTable {
    //...
public:
    //...
    SymValue operator [] (char*);
    SymValue operator () (char*);
};
```

These two members can be easily defined in terms of FindSym. To cater for error cases (i.e., application of the operators to symbols not currently in the table) we assume that no symbol can have the value 0, and return this value for undefined symbols.

```
SymValue SymTable::operator [] (char* name)
{
    Symbol* sym = FindSym(name);
    return (sym == 0 ? 0 : sym->value);
} /* operator [] */

SymValue SymTable::operator () (char* name)
{
    Symbol* sym = FindSym(name);
    return (sym == 0 ? 0 : sym->value);
} /* operator () */
```

The operators now provide us with a more elegant syntax for searching a table.

```
SymTable tab;
//...
cout << tab["alternative"];
cout << tab("alternative");
```

EXERCISE 4.4   *solution provided*

   Define a matrix class together with overloaded operators for matrix arithmetic, as
   suggested below.

```
class Matrix {
      short   rows, cols;
      double *elems;       // matrix elements
public:
              Matrix (short rows,short cols);
              ~Matrix ();
      double  operator () (short row,short col);
      void    SetElem (short row,short col,double val);
      friend  Matrix operator + (Matrix p,Matrix q);
      friend  Matrix operator - (Matrix p,Matrix q);
      friend  Matrix operator * (Matrix p,Matrix q);
      void    Print ();
};
```

4.7 Summary

A function (global or member) is **overloaded** by writing a number of definitions
for it, all of which must be different in terms of the number or type of arguments
they take. For global functions, the definitions must be preceded by an `overload`
declaration.

The predefined **operators** of C++ can be overloaded by defining their new roles as
members or friends of a class. The arity and precedence of an operator cannot be
changed.

Constructors can be used for type conversion from a built-in type to a user-
defined type. Conversion from a user-defined type to a built-in type is facilitated
by overloading the built-in type operator.

References

A reference is very similar to a pointer and is used for introducing an alias for an object. Two major uses of references – passing large objects to functions and returning an lvalue from a function – are discussed. A class, based on the space-efficient implementation of sparse matrices, is then presented to clearly illustrate the power of references. Finally, a comparison between pointers and references is drawn.

5.1 References

A reference introduces a *synonym* for an object. The notation for defining references is similar to that of pointers, except that & is used instead of *. For example,

```
Point  pt1(10,10);
Point& pt2 = pt1;
```

defines pt2 as a reference to pt1. After this definition pt1 and pt2 both refer to the same object, as if they were the same variable. It should be emphasized that a reference does *not* create a copy of an object, but merely a synonym for it. Hence, after

```
pt1.Offset(2,2);
```

both pt1 and pt2 will denote the value (12,12).

A reference must always be initialized as soon as it is defined: it should be a synonym for something. You *cannot* define a reference and initialize it later.

```
Point& pt3;                      // illegal: not initialized
pt3 = pt1;
```

You can also initialize a reference to a constant. In this case a copy of the constant is made (after any necessary type conversion) and the reference is set to refer to the copy.

```
int& i = 1;                      // i refers to a copy of 1
```

The reason that i becomes a reference to a copy of 1 rather than 1 itself is safety. Consider what could happen if this was not the case.

```
int& x = 1;
++x;
int  y = x + 1;
```

The 1 in the first and the 1 in the third line are likely to be the same object (most compilers do constant optimization and allocate both 1's in the same memory location). So although we expect y to be 3, it could turn out to be 4. However, by forcing x to be a copy of 1, the compiler guarantees that the object denoted by x will be different from both 1's.

5.2 Reference arguments

References can be used to define functions that require **variable** parameters. A variable parameter for a function *f* is one which, when changed, causes the corresponding argument in a call to *f* to change as well. This is in contrast to **value** parameters which receive a copy of the corresponding argument in a function call and operate on that copy only. Of course, variable parameters can be simulated by passing pointer arguments, but the use of pointers is not appropriate in all cases.

Recall the overloaded set operators (Section 4.3). Because an overloaded operator cannot operate exclusively on pointers, we had to declare the operands to be of type Set rather than Set*. This is very inefficient because for each use of the operator the operands (entire sets) are copied. References can be used to avoid this. For example, the set intersection operator can be defined as:

```
Set operator * (Set& set1,Set& set2)
{
    Set res;
    for (int i = 0; i < set1.card; ++i)
        for (int j = 0; j < set2.card; ++j)
            if (set1.elems[i] == set2.elems[j]) {
                res.elems[res.card++] = set1.elems[i];
                break;
            }
    return res;
} /* operator * */
```

Some readers may be wondering why we did not also declare the return type of the function as a reference. The reason is that `res` is an automatic variable. When the function returns `res` is destroyed, and any reference to it would be illegal. Unfortunately, if you do this, the compiler will not complain, so some self-discipline is necessary. Should we require `operator*` to return a reference, the proper way of doing it as follows:

```
Set& operator * (Set& set1,Set& set2)
{
    Set* res = new Set;
    for (int i = 0; i < set1.card; ++i)
        for (int j = 0; j < set2.card; ++j)
            if (set1.elems[i] == set2.elems[j]) {
                res->elems[res->card++] = set1.elems[i];
                break;
            }
    return *res;
} /* operator * */
```

By allocating the storage for `res` from the heap, we have ensured that it will not be destroyed when the function returns. However, we have now introduced an additional problem of reclaiming the storage occupied by the return result when it is no longer needed. This style of coding is not really wise. In general, it is much easier to return a copy rather than a reference (as in the first case).

EXERCISE 5.1   *solution provided*

A *bit vector* is a vector with binary elements, that is, each element is either 0 or 1. Small bit vectors can be represented by unsigned integers. For example, an `unsigned char` can represent a bit vector of 8 elements. Larger bit vectors can be defined as arrays of such smaller bit vectors. Complete the definition of the `BitVec` class, as declared below. It should allow bit vectors of any size to be created and manipulated using the associated operators.

```
class BitVec {
     unsigned char* vec;            .        // vector of 8*bytes bits
     short bytes;                            // bytes in the vector
public:
          BitVec   (short dim);             // eg, BitVec(64)
          BitVec   (char* bits);            // eg, BitVec("0011001010110");
        ~BitVec   ()                        { delete vec; }
     Bool    operator [] (short idx);       // retrieve a bit
     void    Set    (short idx);            // set a bit to 1
     void    Reset (short idx);             // reset a bit to 0

     friend  BitVec  operator ~    (BitVec& v);
     friend  BitVec  operator &    (BitVec& v,BitVec& w);
     friend  BitVec  operator |    (BitVec& v,BitVec& w);
     friend  BitVec  operator ^    (BitVec& v,BitVec& w);
     friend  BitVec  operator <<   (BitVec& v,short n);
     friend  BitVec  operator >>   (BitVec& v,short n);
     friend  Bool    operator ==   (BitVec& v,BitVec& w);
     friend  Bool    operator !=   (BitVec& v,BitVec& w);
};
```

5.3 Reference return values

A reference expression is an **lvalue**[1] and hence can appear on both sides of an assignment. If a function returns a reference then a call to that function can be assigned to! This can be used as a valuable programming technique.

To illustrate this, consider the implementation of an associative vector.

```
struct VecElem {
     char* index;
     int    value;
};
```

```
class AssocVec {
     VecElem* elems;     // vector elements
     int dim;            // vector dimension
     int used;           // elements used so far
public:
          AssocVec (int dim);
        ~AssocVec ();
     int  operator [] (char* idx);
};
```

---

[1]   In C jargon, an *lvalue* is anything that denotes the contents of some storage location. For example, if x and p are integer and pointer variables, respectively, then x, *p, * (p+x) are all lvalues.

```
AssocVec::AssocVec (int dim)
{
    AssocVec::dim = dim;
    used = 0;
    elems = new VecElem[dim];
} /* AssocVec */

AssocVec::~AssocVec ()
{
    for (int i = 0; i < used; ++i)
        delete elems[i].index;
    delete elems;
} /* ~AssocVec */

int&
AssocVec::operator [] (char* idx)
{
    for (int i = 0; i < used; ++i)        // search existing elements
        if (strcmp(idx,elems[i].index) == 0)
            return elems[i].value;
    if (used < dim &&                     // create new element
        (elems[used].index = new char[strlen(idx)+1]) != 0) {
        strcpy(elems[used].index,idx);
        elems[used].value = used + 1;
        return elems[used++].value;
    }
    static int dummy = 0;
    return dummy;
} /* operator [] */
```

The overloaded [] operator is used for accessing vector elements. Given a string index, it searches the vector for a match. If a matching index is found then a reference to its associated value is returned. Otherwise, a new element is created, the string is copied to the index of the new element, its value is set to the number of elements in the vector (denoted by used) and a reference to this value is returned. Note that, because the function must return a valid reference, a reference to a dummy static integer is returned when the vector is full or when new fails.

Using AssoVec we can now create associative vectors that behave very much like normal vectors.

```
AssocVec count;
count["apple"] = 5;
count["orange"] = 10;
count["fruit"] = count["apple"] + count["orange"];
```

The example in the next section describes a class that uses references for both passing arguments to functions and for returning values from functions.

5.4 Example: sparse matrices

Finite element analysis [Strang and Fix 1973] is a general numerical method for solving partial differential equations related to various engineering problems (e.g., stress analysis). Using this technique, a partial differential equation is first approximated by a system of linear equations by subdividing the material under consideration into a large number of conceptual partitions (element mesh). Gaussian elimination is then used to solve the system of linear equations. For good accuracy, a fine mesh is required, containing hundreds or even thousands of partitions. Consequently, the resulting system of linear equations may be very large, and coefficient matrices of up to 500*500 are not uncommon. On a machine which uses a 64-bit representation for reals, such a matrix would require 2 megabytes of storage.

Fortunately such matrices are by nature *sparse*: only a few of their elements are nonzero. One can take advantage of this property to produce much more economic representations. One such representation, for example, records only nonzero elements together with their positions in the matrix, where the elements are arranged as a linked-list. Let us define this as a class.

We can represent each element of a matrix as a structure which contains the row and column of the element and its value, plus a pointer to the next element in the linked-list.

```
const minSize = 5;              // minimum number of rows or columns

struct Element {
    short    row, col;
    double   val;
    Element* next;
};
```

The class itself contains the dimensions of the matrix, a pointer to the beginning of the linked-list, a dummy value, and a set of function members for manipulating matrices.

```
class Matrix {
    short    rows, cols;
    Element* elems;              // linked-list of elements
    double   dummy;
    double& InsertElem (Element* elem, short row, short col);
public:
            Matrix (short rows, short cols);
            ~Matrix ();
    short   Rows ()                 { return rows; }
    short   Cols ()                 { return cols; }
    double& operator () (short row, short col);
    friend  Matrix operator + (Matrix&, Matrix&);
    friend  Matrix operator * (Matrix&, Matrix&);
    void    Print ();
};

Matrix::Matrix (short rows, short cols)
{
    Matrix::rows = (rows < minSize ? minSize : rows);
    Matrix::cols = (cols < minSize ? minSize : cols);
    elems = 0;   dummy = 0.0;
} /* Matrix */
```

The private member InsertElem inserts a new element into the linked-list
of elements. Depending on the value of the parameter elem, the new element
may appear before the entry denoted by elem or after it.

```
double& Matrix::InsertElem (Element* elem, short row, short col)
{
    Element* newElem = new Element;
    if (newElem == 0) return dummy;
    newElem->row = row;
    newElem->col = col;
    newElem->val = 0.0;
    if (elem == elems && (elems == 0 || row < elems->row ||
                          row == elems->row && col < elems->col)) {
        newElem->next = elems;
        elems = newElem;
    } else {
        newElem->next = elem->next;
        elem->next = newElem;
    }
    return newElem->val;
} /* InsertElem */
```

To provide a convenient notation for referring to the elements of a matrix, we overload the () operator so that, for example, m(2,3) returns a reference to the element of matrix m in row 2 and column 3. If no such element exists then it is created, its value is initialized to 0.0, and a reference to this value is returned. Otherwise, a reference to the value of the existing element is returned.

```
double& Matrix::operator () (short row, short col)
{
    if (row < 1 || row > rows || col < 1 || col > cols)
        return dummy;
    if (elems == 0 || row < elems->row ||
        row == elems->row && col < elems->col)
        return InsertElem(elems, row, col);
    for (Element* elem = elems; elem->next != 0; elem = elem->next)
        if (row == elem->next->row) {
            if (col == elem->next->col)
                return elem->next->val;
            else if (col < elem->next->col)
                break;
        } else if (row < elem->next->row)
            break;
    return InsertElem(elem, row, col);
} /* operator () */
```

For efficiency reasons, operator() always inserts an element so that the linked-list remains sorted in terms of rows and columns, giving priority to row values.

Since this operator returns a reference, expressions such as m(2,3) are lvalues and can appear on the left-hand side of an assignment. For example, the assignment m(2,3)=10.5 will store 10.5 as the element of m in row 2 and column 3. Using this notation, we can easily define the overloaded operator + for adding two matrices.

```
Matrix operator + (Matrix& p, Matrix& q)
{
    Matrix m(p.rows, q.cols);
    for (Element* pe = p.elems; pe != 0; pe = pe->next)   // copy p
        m(pe->row, pe->col) = pe->val;
    for (Element* qe = q.elems; qe != 0; qe = qe->next)   // add q
        m(qe->row, qe->col) += qe->val;
    return m;
} /* operator + */
```

Printing a matrix is just as easy. We simply iterate through all potential elements of a matrix, printing an element value if it exists, or zero if it does not exist. By taking advantage of the fact that the list is sorted, Print traverses the list only once.

```
void Matrix::Print ()
{
    Element* elem = elems;
    for (short row = 1; row <= rows; ++row) {
        for (short col = 1; col <= cols; ++col)
            if (elem != 0 && elem->row == row && elem->col == col) {
                cout << form("%5.2f ",elem->val);
                elem = elem->next;
            } else
                cout << form("%5.2f ",0.0);
        cout << "\n";
    }
} /* Print */
```

The Matrix class can be tested using a driver which creates two sparse matrices and then prints their sum.

```
main ()
{
    Matrix m(5,5);
    Matrix n(5,5);
    m(2,2) = 1.0;            m(3,3) = 2.0;
    m(4,4) = 3.0;            m(1,1) = 4.0;
    m(1,5) = 5.0;            m(1,3) = 6.0;
    n(2,2) = 10.0;           n(3,3) = 20.0;
    n(3,5) = 30.0;           n(5,2) = 40.0;
    Matrix r = m + n;
    r.Print ();
}
```

This will produce the following output:

```
4.00  0.00   6.00  0.00  5.00
0.00 11.00   0.00  0.00  0.00
0.00  0.00  22.00  0.00 30.00
0.00  0.00   0.00  3.00  0.00
0.00 40.00   0.00  0.00  0.00
```

EXERCISE 5.2   *solution provided*
    Define `operator*` for `Matrix`. Note that, like `operator+`, you do not have to consider all potential elements of two sparse matrices in order to multiply them, but only those which are present.

EXERCISE 5.3   *solution provided*
    Define a destructor for `Matrix`. It should go through the elements in the linked-list and free them one by one.

5.5 References versus pointers

C++ compilers internally implement references as pointers. For example, given the definition

```
int x = 10;
int& xRef = x;
```

the most obvious internal implementation of `xRef` is a pointer to `x` (denoted here by `xPtr`).

```
int* xPtr = &x;
```

Use of `xRef` in expressions causes an implicit dereferencing of `xPtr`.

```
xRef = 20;           // implemented as: *xPtr = 20;
int y = xRef + 5;    // implemented as: y = *xPtr + 5
```

It should then be obvious that references can be used in (almost) every capacity that pointers are used. Given this freedom, the question is: should we do so? The author's opinion is that references should only be used in situations for which they were originally designed (as described in Sections 5.2 and 5.3). In particular, for functions which alter their arguments, the pointer solution is preferred.

```
void Reverse (Element& elem);    // reference version
void Reverse (Element* elem);    // pointer version
```

The reason is that, in the pointer version, the fact that the function may alter its argument is conveniently documented in a call to the function, whereas with the reference version the call gives no such clues.

```
Element elem;
//...
Reverse(elem);                    // call for reference version
Reverse(&elem);                   // call for pointer version
```

More important than whether a programmer prefers the reference version or the pointer version, is consistency. A program which, for the same purpose, sometimes uses the reference style and sometimes the pointer style can be quite confusing.

EXERCISE 5.4   *solution provided*
Can we rewrite the constructor for `Binary` (Section 4.5), declaring its argument as a reference? Why?

5.6 Summary

A **reference** introduces a synonym for an object. Like pointers, there may be many references to a single object at once.

References facilitate **variable** parameters, avoiding the duplication of large objects when they are passed to functions. This is particularly useful for implementing overloaded operators.

A call to a function that returns a **reference value** can be assigned to. This can be used as a valuable programming technique.

Use of **pointers** is preferred over references for passing arguments to a function (but not an operator function) that changes its arguments.

Class Derivation

This chapter describes how a new class is derived from an existing class, without writing the former from scratch, and how a derived class inherits the attributes of its base class. Some simple examples are sketched to illustrate the technique. The presentation of larger examples is deferred to the case studies in Chapters 10-13, which describe some nontrivial classes and derivations thereof.

6.1 Deriving a class

Classes that have much in common are not rare. Defining such classes separately results in considerable duplication of code and is wasteful both in terms of storage and effort. The most natural way of overcoming this difficulty is to have language facilities that can express commonality, so that common parts are written only once and subsequently used to produce as many variants as necessary. C++ has facilities for deriving a new class from an existing class (called a **base** class). The programmer has considerable control over the way a class is derived: the new class can include new members on top of those offered by the base class, hide any of the function members of the base class from the new class, or redefine the functions for the new class.

Let us formulate a simple example around which these issues can be discussed. Consider a class for representing linked-lists of integers.

```
struct Element {
      int      val;
      Element* next;
};
class List {
      Element* elems;
public:
          List ();
          ~List ();
      Bool Insert (int);        // insert in front of list
      Bool Delete (int);        // delete from list
      Bool Contains (int);      // check if in list
};
```

Linked-lists are also suitable for representing sets: a set can be represented by a linked-list from which repeated elements have been removed. Given this commonality, there is no need to define a completely new class for sets; we can derive Set from List.

```
class Set : List {            // derive Set from List
      int card;
      //...
};
```

Set contains everything that List contains and more: card, etc. However, the public members of List are now private in Set. The alternative declaration

```
class Set : public List {
      int card;
      //...
};
```

makes the public members of List also public in Set. It is also possible to specify that only certain public members of a base class be public in a derived class.

```
class Set : List {
      int card;
public:
      List::Contains;
      //...
};
```

Here only Contains is public in Set and all other members of List are private in Set. Note that it is sufficient to simply name such functions; their argument list and return type need not be specified.

6.2 Virtual functions

Unlike Contains, the function members Insert and Delete will have to be redefined for Set, because these may have to adjust card. To facilitate this, we declare them as virtual in the base class and redeclare them in the derived class.

```
class List {                           // base class
     Element* elems;
public:
                List ();
                ~List ();
     virtual Bool Insert (int);
     virtual Bool Delete (int);
            Bool Contains (int);
};
class Set : List {                     // derived class
     int card;
public:
     //...
     Bool Insert (int);
     Bool Delete (int);
};
```

The virtual declarations instruct the compiler that Insert and Delete may have different implementations for classes derived from List. Suppose that these two functions have the following definitions for List.

```
Bool List::Insert (int val)
{
     Element* elem = new Element;
     if (elem != 0) {
          elem->val = val;
          elem->next = elems;
          elems = elem;
     }
     return elem != 0;
} /* Insert */
```

```
Bool List::Delete (int val)
{
    if (elems == 0) return false;        // empty list
    Element* tmp = elems;
    if (elems->val == val) {             // delete the head
        elems = elems->next;
        delete tmp;   return true;
    } else                               // delete from the tail
        for (Element* elem = elems; elem->next != 0; elem = elem->next)
            if (elem->next->val == val) {
                tmp = elem->next;
                elem->next = tmp->next;
                delete tmp;   return true;
            }
    return false;
} /* Delete */
```

Insert and Delete can be redefined for Set.

```
Bool Set::Insert (int val)
{
    if (!Contains(val) && List::Insert(val)) {
        ++card;   return true;
    }
    return false;
} /* Insert */

Bool Set::Delete (int val)
{
    if (List::Delete(val)) {
        --card;   return true;
    }
    return false;
} /* Delete */
```

The latter two functions are defined in terms of the former two. In doing so, we have used the name resolution operator : :. This is necessary because if, for example, we called Delete instead of List::Delete in the definition of Set::Delete, the call would refer to the latter and cause infinite recursion.

For a larger example involving the use of virtual functions see the case study in Chapter 10.

EXERCISE 6.1   *solution provided*

Derive the class SSymTable from the SymTable class (Section 2.3). The derived class should ensure that the entries in each linked-list are alphabetically sorted.

6.3 Access to private part

Neither Set::Insert nor Set::Delete refer to the private part of List. In fact, they cannot; a derived class has no implicit permission to access the private part of its base class. Should such an access be necessary, it can be facilitated by making the relevant members of the derived class (or the entire class) a friend of the base class. The class Set would probably contain many other function members which require access to the private part of List.

```
class Set;                            // forward declaration
class List {
     //...
     friend class Set;
};
class Set : public List {
     int card;
public:
     //...
     Set operator + (Set&);
     Set operator * (Set&);
};
```

Here, operator+ and operator* require access to the private part of List, so Set is declared to be a friend of List. The forward declaration is necessary, since the declaration of Set appears after List, but List refers to Set.

The same effect can be obtained by making only operator+ and operator* friends of List.

```
class Set;
class List {
     //...
     friend Set Set::operator + (Set&);
     friend Set Set::operator * (set&);
};
```

Now Set::operator* has permission to access the private part of List.

```
Set Set::operator * (Set& set)
{
     Set res;
     for (Element* elem = this->elems; elem != 0; elem = elem->next)
          if (set.Contains(elem->val)) res.Insert(elem->val);
     return res;
} /* operator * */
```

The reason that a derived class B is not given implicit permission to access the private part of a base class A is that it would leave A open to the outside world; anyone could access the private part of A by deriving a class from it. This restriction, however, can be removed by specifying the private members of a base class to be protected instead.

```
class List {
protected:
     Element* elems;
public:
     //...
};
```

Any class derived from List will have access to elems and need not be declared a friend of List.

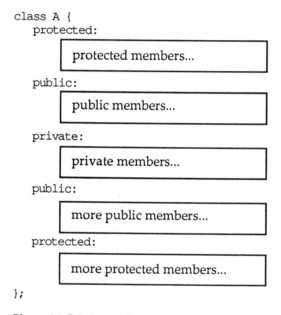

Figure 6.1 Private, public, and protected members.

In general, the keywords private, public, and protected can appear in any order and any number of times in a class, partitioning it into many private, public, and protected parts (see Figure 6.1).

For an example involving the use of protected members see the case study in Chapter 11.

6.4 Constructors and destructors

The `List` class has a constructor and a destructor.

```
inline List::List ()    { elems = 0; }

List::~List ()
{
    Element *elem = elems, *tmp;
    while (elem != 0) {
        tmp = elem;
        elem = elem->next;
        delete tmp;
    }
} /* ~List */
```

These two are applied to `List` and `Set` objects alike. `Set` may also have its own constructor (and destructor).

```
class Set : public List {
    int card;
public:
    Set ()     { card = 0; }
    //...
};
```

When an object of type `Set` is created, the constructors `List::List` and `Set::Set` are applied to it, in that order. When the object name goes out of scope, the destructor `Set::~Set` (if any) and `List::~List` are applied to it, in that order. In other words, for a derived class, the constructors are applied in the order of derivation and the destructors are applied in the opposite order.

The constructor of a derived class whose base class constructor requires arguments should specify these in the definition of its constructor. Here is an example taken from the case study in Chapter 9.

```
class DynMem {                          // base class
    //...
public:
    DynMem (int eps, int wSize);
    //...
};
```

```
class RelMem : DynMem {           // derived class
    //...
public:
    RelMem (int nMas,int eps,int wSize);
    //...
};


RelMem::RelMem (int nMas,int eps,int wSize) : DynMem(eps,wSize)
{
    //...
}
```

RelMem is derived from DynMem. The base class constructor requires two arguments and these are provided by the derived class constructor. This can also be written in an abbreviated form.

```
RelMem::RelMem (int nMas,int eps,int wSize) : (eps,wSize)
{
    //...
}
```

In general, all that a derived class constructor requires is an object from the base class. In some situations, this may not even require referring to the base class constructor.

```
extern DynMem dm;                 // defined elsewhere

RelMem::RelMem (int nMas,int eps,int wSize) : dm
{
    //...
}
```

EXERCISE 6.2   *solution provided*
In Exercise 6.1, suppose that you wish to allow the user to specify that *n* characters in each name are significant, so that Hash will use only the first *n* characters in a name to determine its hash address. Redeclare SSymTable so that this information is supplied to a constructor.

6.5 Example: linear equations

Consider an educational application program which given an arbitrary set of values, $X = [x1, x2, ...,xn]$, generates a set of n linear equations whose solution is X, and then proceeds to illustrate this by solving the equations using Gaussian elimination.

Since Gaussian elimination requires matrix manipulation, we can make use of the Matrix class (Section 5.4). To do so, we define a new class named LinEqns as a derivation of Matrix.

```
class LinEqns : public Matrix {
        int     nEqns;          // number of equations
        double* solution;       // the solution vector
    public:
            LinEqns (int n,double* soln);
            ~LinEqns ()                          { delete solution; }
        void Generate (int coef);
        void Solve ();
};
```

The constructor takes, as arguments, a solution vector and its size. Gaussian elimination requires an $n*(n+1)$ augmented matrix. The derived class constructor should call the base class constructor and pass this information to it.

```
LinEqns::LinEqns (int n,double* soln) : Matrix(n,n+1)
{
    nEqns = n;
    solution = new double[n];
    for (int i = 0; i < n; ++i)
        solution[i] = soln[i];
} /* LinEqns */
```

Generate takes a positive number as argument and generates a set of equations, ensuring that the range of the coefficients does not exceed coef. Coefficients are generated using the UNIX random number generator random and using time as the random seed. Each matrix row denotes one equation. The last element of a row k denotes the right-hand side of the k-th equation and is calculated using the formula

$$M[k,n+1] = \sum_{i=1}^{n} M[k,i] * X[i]$$

```
void
LinEqns::Generate (int coef)
{
    int mid = coef / 2;
    srandom((int) time(0));              // set random seed
    for (int r = 1; r <= nEqns; ++r) {
        (*this)(r,nEqns+1) = 0.0;         // right-hand side
        for (int c = 1; c <= nEqns; ++c) {
            (*this)(r,c) = (double) (mid - random() % coef);
            (*this)(r,nEqns+1) += (*this)(r,c) * solution[c-1];
        }
    }
} /* Generate */
```

EXERCISE 6.3   *solution provided*

Code the function member LinEqns::Solve. It should solve the equations by reducing the augmented matrix to upper-triangular form and by back-substitution. Solve should display the augmented matrix each time the elements below a pivot are eliminated.

Here is a simple test of the LinEqns class:

```
static double s3[] = {2.0,4.5,1.2};
LinEqns eqn(3,s3);
eqn.Generate(10);
eqn.Print();
eqn.Solve();
```

It produces the following output:

```
-2.00  -4.00   5.00 -16.00
 4.00  -1.00  -2.00   1.10
 4.00  -3.00   1.00  -4.30

eliminated below pivot in column 1
 1.00  -0.25  -0.50   0.28
 0.00  -4.50   4.00 -15.45
 0.00  -2.00   3.00  -5.40

eliminated below pivot in column 2
 1.00  -0.25  -0.50   0.28
 0.00   1.00  -0.89   3.43
 0.00   0.00   1.22   1.47
```

```
eliminated below pivot in column 3
   1.00  -0.25  -0.50    0.28
   0.00   1.00  -0.89    3.43
   0.00   0.00   1.00    1.20

      x[1] = 2
      x[2] = 4.5
      x[3] = 1.2
```

6.6 Summary

A new class can be derived from an existing class. The former is called a **derived class**; the latter is called a **base class**. A derived class can itself be the base class of another derived class.

Insertion of the keyword **public** in the declaration of a derived class (before the name of a base class) makes the public members of that base class also public in the derived class. Otherwise, the public members of the base class are private in the derived class.

A function member of a base class that is declared to be **virtual** may have a different implementation in any of its derived classes. Virtual functions are useful when a derived class wants to change some of the function members of the base class to offer, for example, a different interface to the class.

The private members of a base class can be made accessible to a derived class by declaring the latter a friend of the former, or by declaring the private part of the base class as **protected** instead of private.

Objects of a derived class are **constructed** in the order of the derivation (i.e., the base class constructor is applied first, followed by the derived class constructor) and **destroyed** in the opposite order.

Multiple Inheritance

A derived class can have multiple base classes; this leads to multiple inheritance and is the subject of this chapter. It is illustrated by a matrix class example that uses string values as its row and column indices. Complicated class hierarchies may necessitate the sharing of certain base classes. Use of virtual classes for this purpose is discussed. Finally, the inclusion of objects of one class as data members of another class is detailed, and illustrated by an example.

7.1 Multiple inheritance

When a class B is derived from a class A, B **inherits** some or all of attributes of A. One can derive as many classes as required from any given class, even when the latter is itself a derived class.

```
class A { ... };
class B : A { ... };
class C : A { ... };
class D : B { ... };
class E : B { ... };
```

The result is commonly called a **class hierarchy** and can be diagrammatically represented by a tree (see Figure 7.1).

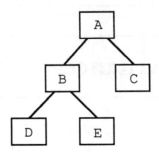

Figure 7.1 Single inheritance.

This form of derivation results in **single inheritance**; each derived class inherits its attributes from exactly one base class. Single inheritance has two main practical applications:

- to generalize/specialize a class by adding attributes to or removing attributes from it, and

- to provide an alternative interface to a class by introducing new function members not offered by the base class, or by redefining such functions.

One can do much with single inheritance alone, but there are also problems whose solution requires a different form of inheritance. Take, for example, a bitmap display-based user interface which offers windows, scroll bars, size boxes, and various forms of buttons, and assume that each of these is supported by a class. Often one wishes to combine two or more of these types to create a new type. For example, it should be possible to combine a window and a scroll bar to produce a scrollable window.

```
class Window {                                      // base class
    //...
public:
    Window (int top, int left, int bottom, int right);
    ~Window ();
};
class ScrollBar {                                   // base class
    //...
public:
    ScrollBar (int top, int left, int bottom, int right);
    ~ScrollBar ();
};
```

```
class ScrollableWind : Window, ScrollBar {      // derived class
    //...
public:
    ScrollableWind (int top, int left, int bottom, int right);
    ~ScrollableWind ();
};
```

As before, ScrollableWind may include new members on top of those offered by Window and ScrollBar. Also, we can make the public members of any of the base classes public in the derived class. For example,

```
class ScrollableWind : public Window, public ScrollBar {
    //...
};
```

makes the public members of Window and ScrollBar public in ScrollableWind.

This form of inheritance (i.e., a derived class inheriting its attributes from more than one base class) is called **multiple inheritance**. Diagrammatically, multiple inheritance can be represented by a graph. Figure 7.2, for example, represents the following class hierarchy.

```
class A { ... };
class B { ... };
class C { ... };
class D : A, B { ... };
class E : B, C { ... };
class F : D, C, E { ... };
```

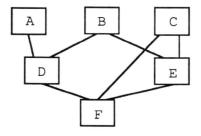

Figure 7.2 Multiple inheritance.

Since the base classes of ScrollableWind have constructors that take arguments, the constructor for the derived class should call these explicitly.

```
ScrollableWind::ScrollableWind (int top,int left,int bottom,int right)
   : Window(top,left,bottom,right),
     ScrollBar(top,right-20,bottom,right)
{    //...
}
```

The order in which the base class constructors are called is the same as the order in which they are nominated by the derived class constructor. In this case, the constructor for Window is called before the constructor for ScrollBar.

In general, a derived class may have any number of base classes. All such classes, however, should be distinct.

```
class X : class A, class B, class A {    // illegal, A appears twice
      //...
};
```

The obvious implementation of a derived class object is to contain one object from each of its base classes.

Multiple inheritance further complicates the rules for referring to the members of a class. For example, suppose that both Window and ScrollBar have a function member called Move for physically moving windows and scroll bars on the screen.

```
class Window {
      //...
public:
      void Move (int x,int y);
};
```

```
class ScrollBar {
      //...
public:
      void Move (int x,int y);
};
```

The derived class ScrollableWind will contain both these functions. As a result, the call

```
ScrollableWind sw;
sw.Move(10,20);
```

is ambiguous and will not compile, because it is not clear whether it refers to

`Window::Move` or `ScrollBar::Move`. The ambiguity is resolved by making the call explicit.

```
sw.Window::Move(10,20);
```

Since moving a scrollable window involves moving both the window and the scroll bar, it is best to have a move function in the derived class which does both.

```
class ScrollableWind : public Window, public ScrollBar {
    //...
public:
    void Move (int x,int y)
            { Window::Move(x,y); ScrollBar::Move(x,y); }
};
```

For any derived class there is an implicit conversion from the derived class to any of its *public* base classes. These can be used for converting derived class object pointers (or references) to base class object pointers (or references).

```
ScrollableWind sw1(10,10,200,200);
Window* w1 = &sw1;              // object pointer conversion
Window& w2 = sw1;              // object reference conversion
```

No such conversion is allowed for objects themselves.

```
Window w3 = sw1;               // error
```

There is no implicit conversion from a base class to a derived class. All such conversions must be explicitly casted.

```
ScrollableWind* sw2 = w1;       // error
ScrollableWind* sw3 = (ScrollableWind*) w1;    // ok
```

For examples involving the casting of class pointers and references see the case study in Chapter 13.

EXERCISE 7.1   *solution provided*

In a bitmap display-based system, files are represented by icons on the screen. Each such icon consists of a 16*16 pixels bitmap and a piece of editable text representing the name of the file. Bitmap and editable text are defined as classes. Derive a class for representing icons and declare a constructor for it.

7.2 Example: a matrix with string indices

Consider the problem of recording the average time required for a message to be transmitted from one machine to another in a long-haul network. This can be represented as a table as illustrated by Figure 7.3.

The row and column indices for this table are strings rather than integers, so the Matrix class (Section 5.4) will not be adequate for representing the table. We need a way of mapping strings to indices. This is already supported by the AssocVec class (Section 5.3). We, therefore, choose to define Table as a derived class of AssocVec and Matrix.

	Sydney	Melbourne	Perth
Sydney	0.00	3.55	12.45
Melbourne	2.34	0.00	10.31
Perth	15.36	9.32	0.00

Figure 7.3 Message transmission time (in seconds).

```
class Table : AssocVec, Matrix {
public:
     Table (int entries);
     double& operator () (char* src, char* dest);
     Matrix::Print;
};


inline
Table::Table (int entries) : AssocVec(entries),
                             Matrix(entries, entries)
{}


inline double&
Table::operator () (char* src, char* dest)
{
     return (*this) ((*this) [src], (*this) [dest]);
}
```

Note that, although the derived class constructor has an empty body, we still have to define it in order to invoke the base class constructors.

The overloaded () operator is used for referring to table entries, and is defined in terms of overloaded [] for AssocVec and overloaded () for Matrix.

We can now set up the table in Figure 7.3 to test this class.

```
Table tab(3);
tab("Sydney",    "Melbourne") = 3.55;
tab("Sydney",    "Perth")    = 12.45;
tab("Melbourne","Sydney")    = 2.34;
tab("Melbourne","Perth")     = 10.31;
tab("Perth",     "Sydney")   = 15.36;
tab("Perth",     "Melbourne") = 9.32;
tab.Print();
```

This will produce the following output:

```
 0.00   3.55  12.45
 2.34   0.00  10.31
15.36   9.32   0.00
```

7.3 Virtual classes

Consider the following three classes:

```
class Port   { /* ... */ };    // graphical drawing port
class Region { /* ... */ };    // arbitrary area on the screen
class Menu   { /* ... */ };    // a set of options
```

Suppose that we have derived two new classes, Window and Palette, from these.

```
class Window: public Port, public Region {
     //...
};
```

```
class Palette: public Port, public Menu {
     //...
};
```

We can proceed by deriving another class, AppWind, from these two.

```
class AppWind: public Window, public Palette {
     //...
};
```

However, since `Port` is a base class for both `Window` and `Palette` it will appear twice in `AppWind`. This may well be desirable. For example, if `AppWind` is intended for application windows that maintain a palette separate from a window then each of these will require its own port (see Figure 7.4). However, if a palette is to be included *inside* a window then both can use the same port (see Figure 7.5).

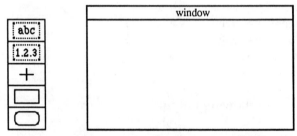

Figure 7.4 Palette and window are physically separate.

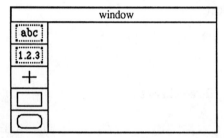

Figure 7.5 Palette is always inside the window.

The latter arrangement is facilitated by making `Port` a `virtual` base class of `Window` and `Palette`. This ensures that an object of type `AppWind` will contain exactly one port. In other words, `Window` and `Palette` will share the same port.

```
class Window: virtual public Port, public Region {
    //...
};

class Palette: virtual public Port, public Menu {
    //...
};
```

A virtual base class must have:

- no constructor, or at least
- a constructor that takes no arguments, or
- a constructor all of whose arguments have default values.

When a derived class object is constructed, the constructors for its virtual base classes are applied first.

For examples involving the use of virtual base classes see the case study in Chapter 13.

7.4 Member objects

A class object can be a data member of another class. Recall the `LinEqns` class (Section 6.5).

```
class LinEqns : public Matrix {
        int     nEqns;
        double* solution;
public:
        LinEqns (int n,double* soln);
        //...
};
```

The data member `solution` is better declared as a `Matrix` of one column rather than a vector of `double`. Similarly, the argument of the constructor is better declared as a `Matrix`.

```
class LinEqns : public Matrix {
        int     nEqns;
        Matrix solution;
public:
        LinEqns (Matrix& soln);
        //...
};
```

If the constructor for a member object, such as `solution`, requires arguments then these must be specified in the definition of the class constructor, in much the same way as arguments are specified for a base class constructor.

```
LinEqns::LinEqns (Matrix& soln) : Matrix(soln.Rows(),soln.Rows()+1),
                                  solution(soln.Rows(),1)
{
        nEqns = soln.Rows();
        for (int i = 1; i <= nEqns; ++i)
            solution(i,1) = soln(i,1);
} /* LinEqns */
```

Here, `LinEqns::LinEqns` invokes both its base class constructor (first call) and the constructor for `solution` (second call), passing arguments to them accordingly. That both cases involve the constructor for `Matrix` is a coincidence.

The specification of arguments for a member object constructor is not necessary if the constructor takes no arguments, or if it has default arguments. Of course, the constructor (if any) is still implicitly called.

Member objects can be used to simulate multiple inheritance. For example, consider deriving a new class `Multiple` from two or more existing classes (`Base1`, `Base2,` and `Base3,` say).

```
class Multiple : Base1, Base2, Base3 {
     //...
};
```

This can be simulated by deriving `Multiple` from one of the base classes and including the rest as member objects in `Multiple`.

```
class Multiple : Base1 {
     Base2 b2;
     Base3 b3;
     //...
};
```

The constructors for `Multiple` have the responsibility of ensuring that the base classes' constructors are properly called. Suppose that the base classes have the following constructors:

```
Base1::Base1 (int k,char* s);
Base2::Base2 (double d);
Base3::Base3 (long n,char* s);
```

A constructor for `Multiple` may look like this:

```
Multiple::Multiple (int n,char* name)
        : Base1(n,name), b2((double)n), b3(n,"a string")
{    //...
}
```

An object m of type `Multiple` is constructed as follows. First the constructor for `Base1` is executed using the argument list `(n, name)`, then `m.b2` and `m.b3` are initialized by the constructors for `Base2` and `Base3` which, respectively, receive `((double)n)` and `(n,"a string")` as argument lists. Finally, the constructor for

`Multiple` is executed. When `m` goes out of scope, it is destroyed in the opposite order: first the destructor for `Multiple` is executed, followed by the destructors for `b2` and `b3`, and finally the destructor for `Base1`.

In general, however, the use of multiple inheritance is preferred as it offers better protection. Data members are used in situations where they cannot be passed as base classes. This is the case when two or more base classes are identical. The `LinEqns` class, for example, involved two matrices, of which one became a base class (object) and the other a member object. The next section describes another typical case where the use of member objects is appropriate.

7.5 More on matrix with string indices

The `Table` class defined in Section 7.2 is only suitable for tables with identical row and column string indices. In some situations this is not adequate.

Consider a table used for storing the number of hours spent by each member of a software development team on different aspects of a software project. An example of this is shown in Figure 7.6 for a project team of 3 people.

	Specification	Design	Coding	Testing
Tim	2.30	3.05	2.45	12.45
Andrew	1.30	5.00	00.30	3.30
Giuseppe	4.30	2.40	10.00	1:30

Figure 7.6 Project time log.

To allow this we have to separate row indices from column indices, that is, use two separate associative vectors. These are conveniently defined as member objects.

```
class Table : Matrix {
      AssocVec rowsVec;
      AssocVec colsVec;
public:
            Table (short rows, short cols);
      double& operator () (char* src, char* dest);
      Matrix::Print;
};
```

```
inline
Table::Table (short rows,short cols)  : Matrix(rows,cols),
                                        rowsVec(rows),
                                        colsVec(cols)

{}


inline double&
Table::operator () (char* src,char* dest)
{
     return (*this)(rowsVec[src],colsVec[dest]);
}
```

EXERCISE 7.2   *solution provided*

Declare two classes Window and Menu which, respectively, represent textual windows and textual menus. The constructor for Window should accept a window's boundary as argument. The constructor for Menu should take a menu owner (a pointer to another menu) as argument. Derive a new class MenuWindow from Window alone. It should record the menu's window, the current option of a menu, and its kind (i.e., one of pull-down or pop-up). Also specify a constructor for the new class.

7.6 Static members

It is possible to declare a data member of a class to be static. This ensures that there will be exactly one copy of the member, shared by all objects of the class. A typical example is a pointer which denotes the list of all existing windows in a window manager.

```
class Window {
     static Window* windList;    // linked-list of all windows
     Window* next;
     //...
};
```

Here, no matter how many objects of type Window are defined, there will be only one windList and this will be initially 0 (all static variables are implicitly initialized to 0). The alternative is to make such variables global, but this is exactly what static members are intended to avoid; by including the variable in a class we can ensure that it will be inaccessible to anything outside the class. Of course, this restriction can be removed by putting such members in the public part of the class.

Unlike global objects, static member objects of a user-defined type cannot receive constructor arguments. For example,

```
class Project {
    static Table timeLog(10,20);      // wrong!
    //...
};
```

is invalid, because timeLog is static but has been given arguments. A reasonable solution here is to provide default arguments for Matrix::Matrix to avoid specifying them explicitly.

That global static objects do not suffer from the same restriction seems rather unreasonable. This, however, is only a limitation of the current implementations of C++, and is likely to be fixed in future releases.

For examples of classes with static members see Sections 8.2 and 8.4. For examples of classes all whose data members are static see Sections 12.3, 13.3, and 13.4.

7.7 Summary

Single inheritance requires a derived class to have exactly one base class. **Multiple inheritance** allows a derived class to have more than one base class.

Virtual classes ensure that duplicate base classes are included only once in a derived class.

A class may contain **objects** of another class. Such objects are constructed in a way similar to base class objects of a derived class. Member objects are used to simulate multiple inheritance when a class directly contains two or more objects of another class.

Data members of a class can be **static**, in which case they are shared by all objects of that class. Static member objects cannot be given constructor arguments.

CHAPTER 8

Pointers and Dynamic Storage

This chapter discusses issues related to the use of pointers and dynamically allocated blocks. Particular attention is paid to the new and delete operators and how they are overloaded. Overloading of other pointer operators is also discussed as well as the use of function pointers in general and pointers to class members in particular. Finally, a safe method for copying objects that involve pointers is presented, and illustrated by an example involving the bit-vector class.

8.1 Dynamic objects

Like objects of a built-in type, objects of a class behave according to their storage category. Static and global objects are created when execution of a program commences and destroyed when the program terminates. Automatic objects are created when the enclosing block is executed, and destroyed when the block is left. Dynamic objects are created using new and destroyed using delete.

When using new for creating an object, the operand to new must take the form of a call to a class constructor. For example,

```
SymTable* tab1 = new SymTable(64);
SymTable* tab2 = new SymTable;
```

are both valid, creating `tab1` and `tab2` dynamically and applying the `SymTable` constructor to them (the latter uses the default argument for the constructor). Similarly,

```
delete tab1;
delete tab2;
```

destroy `tab1` and `tab2`. The class destructor (if any) is applied before the objects are destroyed.

A class constructor can use its own allocation mechanism by creating a block of the required size and assigning its address to `this`. A class destructor can then liberate the block and assign 0 to `this`.

```
SymTable::SymTable (int sz)
{
    this = MyNew(sizeof(SymTable));    // don't use new
    //...
}

SymTable::~SymTable ()
{
    MyDelete(this);   this = 0;        // don't use delete
    //...
}
```

Given this, the effect of `new` and `delete` is similar to calling the constructor and the destructor directly, but will produce an object pointer instead.

```
SymTable* tab = new(16);      // tab is a pointer to the object
SymTable  tab(16);            // same, but tab is the object itself
```

This technique is not recommended as it can be quite misleading. Some C++ compilers do not even allow it. A better way of gaining control over storage allocation is to overload `new` and `delete`. This is discussed in the next section.

Objects are usually created and used individually. In some situations, however, it is desirable to create a whole block (vector or array) of objects. For example, a pentagon can be defined as an array of 5 points.

```
Point pentagon[5];
```

This declaration imposes an important restriction upon the class: `Point` should either have no constructor at all, or at least a constructor that takes *no* arguments whatsoever. Unfortunately, when this is not the case the compiler will not complain.

If we wish to re-initialize the array using a constructor that does take arguments, we can always apply it manually.

```
class Point {
    //...
public:
    Point ();
    Point (int,int);
};

Point pentagon[5];
pentagon[0].Point(5,10);
pentagon[1].Point(2,2);
pentagon[2].Point(10,20);
//...
```

In this case, pentagon is initialized twice, once by either constructor.

An array of objects can also be created dynamically using new.

```
Point* pentagon = new Point[5];
```

However, in this case, the dimension of the array must also be given when destroying it using delete.

```
delete[5] pentagon;
```

Dynamic object arrays as such are useful in circumstances where we cannot predetermine the size of the array. For example, a general polygon class has no way of knowing in advance how many vertices a polygon may have.

```
class Polygon {
    Point* vertices;        // the vertices
    int     nVertices;      // the number of vertices
public:
    //...
};
```

8.2 Overloading new and delete

New and delete are externally defined library functions. Like many other library functions, their external declaration is automatically included when a C++ program is compiled.

```
extern void* operator new (long bytes);
extern void  operator delete (void* ptr);
```

The parameter of new specifies the number of bytes to be allocated. But recall that when using new we give it a *type* as operand rather than a block size. The compiler works out the size automatically from the type.

The memory management strategy employed by new and delete is a general one and is adequate for most applications. In some situations, however, total control over memory management may be necessary, for example, to ensure better efficiency or overcome limitation imposed by the target machine. This is facilitated by overloading new and delete.

New and delete can be overloaded in two ways: either globally, in which case they override the default definitions; or locally for a class, in which case the overloaded versions apply to that class only.

To globally overload new and delete, we redefine them as external in the global scope. (Recall that new and delete are overloaded by default, hence no overload declaration is necessary.)

```
extern void*
operator new (long bytes)
{
    // algorithm to allocate a block from some memory space
    // new should return a void* pointer to the beginning of the block
}

extern void
operator delete (void* ptr)
{
    // algorithm to free the block pointed to by ptr
}
```

Exactly what algorithm to use depends on the application. In some cases, a simple strategy based on allocating blocks from a static array may be sufficient. In other cases, a sophisticated strategy which uses the memory management facilities of the host operating system may be desirable. (See the case study in Chapter 10 for a sample algorithm.)

Overloading new and delete for specific classes is more common. This is because different classes have often very different structures and impose different memory requirements. As a result, they cannot be optimally served by one global strategy.

Small objects, in particular, are not efficiently handled by the default versions of new and delete. Every block allocated by new carries some overhead used for housekeeping purposes. For large objects this is not significant, but for small objects the overhead may be even bigger than the block itself. In addition, having too many small blocks can severely slow down subsequent allocation and deallocation. The performance of a program that dynamically creates many small objects can be significantly improved by using a simpler memory management strategy for those objects.

Every Point object, for instance, consists of only two integers. If a program creates a few hundred points using new then it makes sense to overload new and delete for Point and allocate storage from a static array.

```
const  maxPoints = 512;
class Point {
    int xVal, yVal;

    static union Block {
        int     xy[2];
        Block* next;
    } blocks[maxPoints];        // static array of blocks
    static Block* freeList;     // free list of linked blocks
    static int used;            // blocks used so far
public:
    //...
    void* operator new (long bytes);
    void  operator delete (void* ptr);
};
```

Since blocks, freeList and used are static they do not affect the size of a Point object (it is still two integers). New takes the next available block from blocks and returns its address. Delete frees a block by inserting it in front of the linked-list denoted by freeList. When used reaches maxPoints, free removes and returns the first block in the linked-list, but fails (returns 0) when the linked-list is empty.

```
void*
Point::operator new (long bytes)
{
    Block* res = freeList;
    return used < maxPoints
                ? & (blocks [used++])
                : (res == 0 ? 0 : (freeList = freeList->next, res));
} /* new */

void
Point::operator delete (void* ptr)
{
    ((Block*) ptr)->next = freeList;
    freeList = (Block*) ptr;
} /* delete */
```

`Point::new` and `Point::delete` are invoked *only* for `Point` objects. Calling `new` with any other type as argument will invoke the global definition of `new`, even if the call occurs inside a function member of `Point`.

```
Point* pt = new Point(1,1);     // calls Point::operator new
char*  str = new char[10];      // calls ::operator new
```

8.3 Storage economy

Programs which use a very large number of dynamic blocks can become hopelessly inefficient, spending most of their time doing memory management. In such cases one should try to reduce the number of calls to `new` as much as possible. We present two examples of how this can be done.

Consider the following class for representing a person, having 3 data members.

```
class Person {
    char* name;
    int   age;
    Sex   sex;
    //...
};
```

Dynamic allocation of an object of type `Person` usually involves two calls to `new`, one for the object and one for the pointer denoted by name. These two calls can be combined into one by a slight modification of the class.

```
class Person1 {
    int    age;
    Sex    sex;
    char   name[1];                // the first char in a name
    //...
};
```

Name has been moved to become the last data member of the class and its declaration has been changed to an array of one character. To allocate an object of type Person1, we calculate the total size for the object and the name and request a block of that size.

```
char* aName = "Michael";
Person1* p = (Person1*) new char[sizeof(Person1) + strlen(aName)];
strcpy(p->name,aName);
```

The economy is gained at a price: the code is now less readable, and changing a person's name is now more difficult. In this case, however, it is acceptable because a person is unlikely to change his name. (See Section 10.2 and 12.7 for other examples of this form of allocation.)

If we were to construct a vector of n Person objects, we could economize even further. Suppose that the data is given to us in three separate arrays, one for names (nameVec), one for ages (ageVec), and one for sexes (sexVec).

```
int totLen = 0, i;
for (i = 0; i < n; ++i)                 // calculate total length of names
    totLen += strlen(nameVec[i]) + 1;
Person* perVec = new Person[n];         // allocate Person vector
char* names = new char[totLen];         // allocate one long names block
for (i = 0; i < n; ++i) {               // copy data to perVec
    perVec[i].name = names;             // set the name address
    strcpy(perVec[i].name,nameVec[i]);  // copy name
    names += strlen(nameVec[i]);        // set names to point to next name
    perVec[i].age = ageVec[i];
    perVec[i].sex = sexVec[i];
}
```

Each name, therefore, is a pointer to a portion of a large block that contains all the names (denoted by names). This reduces the number of calls to new from $n+1$ to 2.

It is not altogether a safe approach, though. A destructor for `Person`, for example, should be coded very carefully, or the job of destruction should be handed over to another class. (See Section 12.6 for a safe example of this form of allocation.)

8.4 Overloading ->, *, and &

It is possible to divert the flow of control to a user-defined routine before a pointer to an object is dereferenced using `->` or `*`, or before the address of an object is obtained using `&`. This can be used to do some extra pointer processing, and is facilitated by overloading unary operators `->`, `*`, and `&`.

For classes that do not overload `->`, this operator is binary: the left operand is a pointer to a class object and the right operand is a class member name. For a class X that overloads `->`, the operator is treated as unary. In this case, `->` is first applied to its left operand to produce a pointer result p. Assuming that the result is a pointer to a class Y, if Y does not overload `->` then p is used as the left operand of binary `->`. Otherwise, p is used as the left operand of unary `->` and the whole procedure is repeated for class Y. Consider the following classes that overload `->`:

```
class A {
    //...
    B* operator -> ();
};

class B {
    //...
    Point* operator -> ();
};
```

The effect of dereferencing a pointer to an object of type A

```
A* aPtr = new A;
int i = aPtr->xVal;            // dereferencing aPtr
```

is the successive application of overloaded `->` in A and B.

```
int i = (B::operator->(A::operator->(aPtr)))->xVal;
```

In other words, `A::operator->` is applied to `aPtr` to give p, `B::operator->` is applied to p to give q, and since q is a pointer to `Point`, the final result is `q->xVal`.

Unary operators `*` and `&` can also be overloaded so that the semantic correspondence between `->`, `*`, and `&` is preserved.

As an example, consider a library system which represents a book record as a raw string of the following format:

"%Aauthor\0%Ttitle\0%Ppublisher\0%Ccity\0%Vvolume\0%Yyear\0\n"

Each field starts with a field specifier (e.g., %A specifies an author) and ends with a null character (i.e., \0). The fields can appear in any order. Also, some fields may be missing from a record, in which case a default value must be used.

For efficiency reasons we may want to keep the data in this format but use the following structure whenever we need to access the fields of a record.

```
struct Book {
      char* raw;                      // raw format (kept for reference)
      char* author;
      char* title;
      char* publisher;
      char* city;
      short vol;
      short year;
};
```

The default field values are denoted by a global Book variable.

```
Book defBook = {
      "raw", "Author?", "Title?", "Publisher?", "City?", 0, 0
};
```

We now define a class for representing raw records, and overload the unary pointer operators to map a raw record to a Book structure whenever necessary.

```
class RawBook {
      char* data;
      static Book  cache[10];     // cache memory
      static short curr;          // current record in cache
      static short used;          // number of used cache records
      Book* RawToBook ();
public:
            RawBook (char* str)      { data = str; }
      Book* operator -> ();
      Book& operator * ();
      Book* operator & ();
};
```

To reduce the frequency of mappings from RawBook to Book, we have used a simple cache memory of 10 records. The private function RawToBook searches the cache for a RawBook and returns a pointer to its corresponding Book structure. If the book is not in the cache, RawToBook loads the book at the current position in the cache.

```cpp
Book*
RawBook::RawToBook ()
{
        char* str = data;
        for (int i = 0; i < used; ++i)             // search cache
            if (data == cache[i].raw)
                 return cache + i;
        curr = used < 10 ? used++                  // update curr and used
                    : (curr < 9 ? ++curr : 0);
        Book* bk = cache + curr;                   // the book
        *bk = defBook;                             // set default values
        bk->raw = data;
        for (;;) {
            while (*str++ != '%')                  // skip to next specifier
                ;
            switch (*str++) {                      // get a field
                case 'A': bk->author = str;    break;
                case 'T': bk->title  = str;    break;
                case 'P': bk->publisher = str; break;
                case 'C': bk->city = str;      break;
                case 'V': bk->vol = atoi(str); break;
                case 'Y': bk->year = atoi(str); break;
            }
            while (*str++ != '\0')                 // skip till end of field
                ;
            if (*str == '\n') break;               // end of record
        }
        return bk;
} /* RawToBook */
```

The overloaded operators ->, *, and & are easily defined in terms of RawToBook.

```cpp
Book* RawBook::operator -> ()   { return RawToBook(); }
Book& RawBook::operator *  ()   { return *RawToBook(); }
Book* RawBook::operator &  ()   { return RawToBook(); }
```

The identical definitions for -> and & should not be surprising since -> is unary in this context and semantically equivalent to &.

The following test case demonstrates that the operators behave as expected. It sets up two book records and prints each using different operators.

```
main ()
{
    RawBook r1 ("%ATanenbaum\0%TComputer Networks\0%PPrentice Hall\0
               %CEnglewood Cliffs, NJ\0%Y1981\0\n");
    RawBook r2 ("%TSoftware Engineering\0%ASteward\0%Y1987\0
               %PBrooks/Cole\0\n");
    cout << r1->author    << ", " << r1->title    << ", "
         << r1->publisher << ", " << r1->city     << ", "
         << (*r1).vol     << ", " << (*r1).year    << "\n";
    Book* bp = &r2;            // note use of &
    cout << bp->author    << ", " << bp->title    << ", "
         << bp->publisher << ", " << bp->city     << ", "
         << bp->vol       << ", " << bp->year     << "\n";
}
```

It produces the following output:

```
Tanenbaum, Computer Networks, Prentice Hall, Englewood Cliffs, NJ, 0, 1981
Steward, Software Engineering, Brooks/Cole, City?, 0, 1987
```

8.5 Function pointers

It is possible to take the address of a function and store it in a function pointer. The pointer can then be used to call the function.[1] For example,

```
int (*Compare) (char*,char*);
```

declares a function pointer named Compare which can hold the address of any function that takes two character pointers as arguments and returns an integer.

```
Compare = &strcmp;
```

A function pointer is usually passed as argument to another function; typically because the latter requires different versions of the former in different circumstances. A good example is a binary search routine for searching a sorted

---

[1]   Function pointers are also supported by C.

array of items. By passing the comparison function as an argument to the search routine, we can make the latter independent of the type of items stored in the array.

```
int
BinSearch (void* item, void** table, int n, int (*Compare) (void*, void*))
{
    int bot = 0, top = n - 1, mid, cmp;
    while (bot <= top) {
        mid = (bot + top) / 2;
        if ((cmp = (*Compare) (item, table [mid])) == 0)
            return mid;                 // return item index
        else if (cmp < 0)
            top = mid - 1;
        else
            bot = mid + 1;
    }
    return -1;                          // not found
}
```

By specifying void* as the type of each item and the type of arguments to Compare, we can avoid much unnecessary type casting. Here is a sample call to BinSearch which uses the standard string comparison function strcmp.

```
char* tab[] = {"abort", "bull", "cart", "dull", "wall"};
cout << BinSearch ("dull", (void**) tab, 5, &strcmp) << "\n";
```

Regardless of the type of items stored in the array, BinSearch will work, provided it is given an appropriate comparison function.

```
struct Record {
    int    key;
    char* name;
    void* attributes;
}* records [100];

inline int
KeyCompare (Record* r1, Record* r2)     { return r1->key - r2->key; }

//...
Record dummy;
dummy.key = 10229;
int index = BinSearch (&dummy, (void**) record, 100, &KeyCompare);
```

Having a pointer to a function member is slightly more complicated. In this case, the class name should also be included in the function type. The following example stores the address of the RmvSym function member (Chapter 2) in a pointer variable (fun) and then calls RmvSym via the pointer.

```
SymTable tab1, *tab2;
//...
typedef Bool (SymTable::*MyFun)(char*);    // function pointer type
MyFun fun = &SymTable::RmvSym;             // function pointer
(tab1.*fun)("block");                      // call RmvSym for tab1
(tab2->*fun)("block");                     // call RmvSym for tab2
```

The same syntax can be used for data member pointers. The following example will work provided size is a public member of SymTable or the code appears inside one of the function members.

```
int SymTable::*sz;              // pointer to an int data member
sz = &SymTable::size;          // set it to point to size
int n = tab1.*sz;              // get size of tab1
int m = tab2->*sz;            // get size of tab2
```

The same protection rules still apply: to take the address of a class member (data or function) one should have access to it. For example, a function which does not have access to the private part of a class cannot take the address of any of the private members of the class.

8.6 Object copying

Like objects of built-in types, objects of user-defined types are copied in the following situations:

- To create and initialize an object in a declaration that uses another object as its initializer, e.g., Point q = p in Foo below.
- To copy an object in an assignment, e.g., p = r in Foo below.
- To pass an object argument to a function (not applicable to a reference or pointer argument), e.g., p in Foo below.
- To return an object value from a function (not applicable to a reference or pointer return value), e.g., return r in Foo below.

```
Point Foo (Point p)              // bitwise copy an argument to p
{
        Point q = p;             // bitwise copy p to q
        Point r(10,20);
        p = r;                   // bitwise copy r to p
        //...
        return r;                // bitwise copy r and return copy
}
```

All such copying is **bitwise**, that is, after copying, both objects have exactly the same bit pattern. This is fine for objects such as `Point`, all whose data members are integers. In contrast, bitwise copying of objects that contain pointers can be very dangerous. Consider the `BitVec` class (Exercise 5.1).

```
class BitVec {
        unsigned char* vec;      // vector of 8*bytes bits
        short bytes;             // bytes in the vector
public:
        //...
};
```

Each `BitVec` object contains two components, one of which (`vec`) is a pointer. Now consider the effect of the following function:

```
Foo ()
{
        BitVec v(128);
        BitVec w = v;
        //...
}
```

When `Foo` is called, v and w are created. The former is initialized by a `BitVec` constructor, while the later is initialized by a bitwise copy from v to w. As a result, `v.vec` and `w.vec` point to the same dynamic block. This will cause very strange behavior. For example, after

```
v.Set (15);
```

both v and w will have their 15th bit set to 1. But that is not all; the worst happens when `Foo` returns. At this point the destructor `BitVec::~BitVec` is applied to both v and w, attempting to release `v.vec` twice!

It should then be obvious that bitwise copying is not adequate for objects that contain pointers. What we need is a means of **structurally** copying such objects and recreating the blocks denoted by pointers. In C++, this is facilitated for a class X by providing it with two special members:

- A constructor of the form X::X(X& x). It should create an object like other constructors, but use x for initializing the object.

- An overloaded X& X::operator=(X& x) which structurally copies x to the objects for which it is invoked.

It should be emphasized that, to cater for all copying situations, *both* these must be provided. For the BitVec class, for example, this is done as follows.

```cpp
class BitVec {
        unsigned char* vec;
        short bytes;
public:
                BitVec   (short dim);
                BitVec   (char* bits);
        //...
                BitVec   (BitVec& v);          // special constructor
        BitVec&  operator = (BitVec& v);       // special operator =
};

BitVec::BitVec (BitVec& v)
{
        bytes = v.bytes;
        vec = (unsigned char*) new char[bytes];
        for (int i = 0; i < bytes; ++i)        // copy bytes
                vec[i] = v.vec[i];
} /* BitVec */

BitVec&
BitVec::operator = (BitVec& v)                 // assignment
{
        for (int i = 0; i < (v.bytes < bytes ? v.bytes : bytes); ++i)
                vec[i] = v.vec[i];             // copy bytes
        for (; i < bytes; ++i)                 // extra bytes in *this
                vec[i] = 0;
        return *this;
} /* operator = */
```

Given these extra members, declaring a BitVec as a copy of another BitVec and assigning one BitVec to another work properly.

```
Foo ()
{
    BitVec v(128);        // initialized by BitVec::BitVec(short)
    BitVec w = v;         // initialized by BitVec::BitVec(BitVec&)
    BitVec y("0110010");  // initialized by BitVec::BitVec(char*)
    v = y;                // assigned by BitVec::operator=(BitVec&)
    //...
}
```

The destruction of v, w, and y upon Foo returning works correctly too, because they denote three separate objects whose vec parts are distinct.

Structural copying, when defined, is implicitly applied by the compiler in all the situations mentioned earlier for bitwise copying. These are reiterated below.

- To create and initialize an object in a declaration that uses another object as its initializer, e.g., Point w = v in Foo.
- To copy an object in an assignment, e.g., v = y in Foo.
- To pass an object argument to a function (not applicable to a reference or pointer argument).
- To return an object value from a function (not applicable to a reference or pointer return value).

We should stress that operator= is best defined as a member of a class rather than a friend. This ensures that unwanted type conversions will not take place. For example, had we defined operator= as a friend of BitVec,

```
BitVec v("00000011");
"01101011" = v;
```

would be valid and would cause "01101011" to be implicitly converted to an object of type BitVec (this is because BitVec has a constructor of type BitVec::BitVec(char*) – see Section 4.4) and v copied to this object. The object would then be destroyed, so the overall effect is nothing at all! However, given that operator= is a member of BitVec and not a friend, the above assignment will be rejected by the compiler.

Structural copying is also applicable to member objects and derived classes. Consider the following class which contains a BitVec member.

```
class Device {
    int    devNum;              // device number
    BitVec status;              // device status bits
    char   buffer[256];         // device buffer
public:
            Device (int dn,short nStat);
            Device (Device& dev);        // not really needed
    Device& operator = (Device& dev);    // not really needed
    //...
};

Device::Device (int dn,short nStat) : status(nStat)  { devNum = dn; }
Device::Device (Device& dev) : status(dev.status)     {}

Device&
Device::operator = (Device& dev)
{
    devNum = dev.devNum;
    status = status;                // structural copy
    for (int i = 0; i < 256; ++i)
        buffer[i] = dev.buffer[i];
    return *this;
} /* operator = */
```

We can provide special members for structurally copying status as shown here.
This is, however, unnecessary. If not defined, the compiler automatically
generates Device::Device(Device&) and Device::operator=(Device&) for us. In
either case, when an object of type Device is copied (in an assignment, for
example) the components devNum and buffer are bitwise copied and status is
structurally copied.

The same rules apply when Device is defined as a derived class of BitVec,
causing the compiler to automatically define the two members for structural
copying.

```
class Device1 : public BitVec {
    int    devNum;              // device number
    char   buffer[256];         // device buffer
public:
    Device1 (int dn,short nStat) : BitVec(nStat)  { devNum = dn; }
    //...
};
```

However, should `Device` or `Device1` contain pointer members (as `BitVec` did) then it would make sense to define structural-copying members to handle them.

```
class Device2 : public BitVec {
        int     devNum;                    // device number
        char*   buffer;                    // device buffer (a pointer)
    public:
                Device2 (int dn, short bufSize, short nStat);
                Device2 (Device2& dev);
        Device2& operator = (Device2& dev);
        //...
};
```

EXERCISE 8.1   *solution provided*
Overload the `&=`, `|=`, `^=`, `<<=`, and `>>=` operators as members of `BitVec`. Note that these can be easily defined in terms of the earlier operators and `=`.

8.7 Example: enumeration sets

We have seen the use of special constructors such as `BitVec::BitVec(BitVec&)`. Deriving a class from `BitVec` may necessitate another form of constructor which also takes a `BitVec&` argument. The example in this section illustrates one such case.

Enumerations introduced by an `enum` declaration are small subsets of integers. In certain applications we may need to construct sets of such enumerations. For example, in a parser, each parsing routine may be passed a set of symbols that should not be skipped when the parser attempts to recover from a syntax error. These symbols are typically the reserved words of the language.

```
enum Reserved {classSym, privateSym, publicSym, protectedSym,
               friendSym, ifSym, thenSym, elseSym, switchSym, ...};
```

The `Set` class (Section 4.3) would be too inefficient for representing sets of such symbols. Given that there may be at most n elements in a set (n being a small number) the set can be efficiently represented as a bit vector of n elements. This is facilitated by deriving a new class from `BitVec` and overloading the set operators for it.

```
class EnumSet : public BitVec {
public:
            EnumSet (short maxCard) : BitVec(maxCard) {}
            EnumSet (BitVec& v) : BitVec(v)   { *this = (EnumSet&)v; }
    friend  EnumSet  operator +  (EnumSet& s,EnumSet& t);
    friend  EnumSet  operator -  (EnumSet& s,EnumSet& t);
    friend  EnumSet  operator *  (EnumSet& s,EnumSet& t);
    friend  Bool     operator %  (short elem,EnumSet& s);
    friend  Bool     operator <= (EnumSet& s,EnumSet& t);
    friend  Bool     operator >= (EnumSet& s,EnumSet& t);
    friend  EnumSet& operator << (EnumSet& s,short elem);
    friend  EnumSet& operator >> (EnumSet& s,short elem);
};
```

The `EnumSet` operators are easily defined in terms of `BitVec` operators. For example, the union operator + in `EnumSet` is the same as the bitwise "or" operator | in `BitVec`.

```
inline EnumSet
operator + (EnumSet& s,EnumSet& t)    {return s | t;}    // union

inline EnumSet
operator - (EnumSet& s,EnumSet& t)    {return s & ~t;}   // difference

inline EnumSet
operator * (EnumSet& s,EnumSet& t)    {return s & t;}    // intersection
```

Note the type conversions. In

```
return s | t;
```

both s and t are of type `EnumSet &` and are implicitly converted by the compiler to the base type `BitVec&` to match the operand types of | (see Section 7.1). The result of this operation is of type `BitVec` and needs to be converted to `EnumSet` to match the return type of +. This type conversion is performed by the constructor `EnumSet::EnumSet(BitVec&)`.

For `EnumSet` this is the most appropriate way of handling the type conversion from the base class to the derived class. Explicit casting of the form

```
return (EnumVec) (s | t);
```

will not work because conversion between base and derived classes works for object pointers and references, but not the objects themselves.

EXERCISE 8.2   *solution provided*
> Give definitions for the remaining operators in EnumSet: % returns true if its first operand is a member of its second operand, <= and >= test for one set being a subset of another set, >> inserts an element into a set, and << removes an element from a set.

8.8 Summary

Dynamic objects are created using new and destroyed using delete. As before, constructors and destructors are implicitly applied to such objects.

New and delete can be redefined **globally**, or overloaded **locally** for a given class. The latter is suitable for classes that do their own memory management.

Unary operators ->, *, and & can be overloaded for pointer manipulation in a class. This is useful for gaining control over the way pointers to class objects are produced or dereferenced.

The address of a function (or function member) can be stored in a variable. The latter is called a **function pointer** and may be used to call the function.

Object copying is **bitwise** by default. This is inappropriate for objects that contain pointers.

Structural copying of objects that contain pointers is facilitated by defining a special constructor that takes a class reference as argument, and by overloading the assignment operator.

Objects of a class for which structural copying is defined obey structural copying even when they are used as members in another class or as a base class.

Other Facilities

This chapter describes the remaining facilities of C++ not covered by the earlier chapters. Some of these facilities (e.g., constants and streams) have already been introduced superficially; they are described here in more detail. C++ constants and functions with variable number of arguments are directly borrowed from ANSI C [Kernighan and Ritchie 1988]. The role of these facilities in relation to classes is discussed. Other topics include structures and nested class declarations, the use of generic classes, and the I/O facilities of C++.

9.1 Constants and enumerations

Preceding a variable declaration by the keyword const makes that variable read-only (i.e., a constant). A constant must be initialized to some value when it is defined.

```
const int maxSize = 128;
const double pi = 3.141592654;
const int powersOf2[] = {1,2,4,8,16,32,64,128};
```

Once defined, the value of a constant cannot be changed.

```
maxSize = 256;              // wrong
powersOf2[0] = 0;           // wrong
```

The constants used in earlier chapters had no type specifiers. All such constants are taken to be integers.

```
const maxSize = 128;            // maxSize is of type int
```

With pointers, two aspects need to be considered: the pointer itself, and the object pointed to, either of which or both can be constant.

```
const char* str1 = "pointer to constant";
char* const str2 = "constant pointer";
const char* const str3 = "constant pointer to constant";
str1[0] = 'P';                  // wrong
str1 = "ptr to const";          // ok
str2 = "const ptr";             // wrong
str2[0] = 'P';                  // ok
str3 = "const to const ptr";    // wrong
str3[0] = 'C';                  // wrong
```

A function argument may also be declared to be constant. This is useful for functions that take pointer or reference arguments for efficiency reasons and never alter the object denoted by the argument.

```
int strlen (const char* str)  { ... }
Set Operator * (const Set& set1, const Set& set2)  { ... }
```

A function may also return a constant result.

```
const char* SystemVersion ()  { ... }
```

An enumeration of constants is introduced by an enum declaration. This is useful for declaring a set of closely-related constants.

```
enum {north, south, east, west};
```

All such constants are of type int and, unless specified otherwise, have successive values starting from 0. Here, for example, north is 0, south is 1, etc. This can be overruled by explicit initialization.

```
enum {north = 10, south, east = 0, west};
```

Here, south is 11 and west is 1. An enumeration can also be named, where the name becomes an alias for int.

```
enum Direction {north, south, east, west};
Direction d;                      // declares d to be of type int
```

Enumerations are particularly useful for naming the cases of a switch statement.

```
switch (d) {
      case north:   //...
      case south:   //...
      case east:    //...
      case west:    //...
}
```

A constant or enumeration declaration can be local to a class. The following example is taken from a class in Section 11.2.

```
class DynMem {
      enum  Status {vacant,used};
      const maxHeap = 16384;
      //...
};
```

The syntax for referring to Status, vacant, used, and maxHeap is the same as for other data members of the class. They also obey the same scope and protection rules. Here, for example, all are private and inaccessible outside the class. As with static members (Section 7.6), enumerations and constants do not affect the size of a class.

9.2 Structures and classes

In C++, a struct is a class all of whose members are public. Like a class, therefore, it can include both data and function members.

```
struct Point {                    // this is...
      int x, y;
      void Point (int,int);
      void OffsetPt (int,int);
};
```

```
class Point {                    // ...equivalent to this
public:
    int x, y;
    void Point (int,int);
    void OffsetPt (int,int);
};
```

The declaration of a structure or a class can appear inside another.[1] For example, we can declare a new class, Rectangle, which in turn contains the declaration of Point.

```
class Rectangle {                // a nested class
    class Point {
        int x, y;
    public:
        Point (int,int);
        void OffsetPt (int,int);
    };
    Point topLeft, botRight;
public:
    Rectangle (Point,Point);
    void OffsetRect (int,int);
};
```

Unlike constants and enumerations, a structure/class declaration that appears inside another structure/class is *not* local to the latter. Here, for example, Point can still be used as if it were declared outside Rectangle. As a result, the following function is perfectly valid.

```
main ()
{
    Point pt1 (10,10);
    Point pt2 (20,20);
    Rectangle rect (pt1,pt2);
    //...
}
```

This inconsistency is rather unfortunate and certainly a flaw in the design of the language. Nested classes appear to be useful only in one situation: when a class B is used by only another class A. A nested class can document this fact, but the compiler will not enforce it.

---

[1] This equally applies to unions; we have already used it in an example. See the Point class in Section 8.2.

9.3 Variable number of arguments

It is often useful, if not necessary, to have functions which take a variable number of arguments. A simple example is a function which takes a set of menu options as arguments, displays the menu, and allows the user to choose one of the options. To be general, the function should be able to accept any number of options as arguments. In C++ (and ANSI C) this is expressed as

```
int Menu (char* option1 ...);
```

which says that Menu should be given at least one argument and possibly more.

Menu can access its arguments using a set of macros defined in the header file stdarg.h and may be coded as follows (the macros appear in **bold**):

```
#include <stream.h>
#include <stdarg.h>

int Menu (char* option1 ...)
{
    va_list args;                  // argument list
    char*    option = option1;
    int      count = 0, choice = 0;
    va_start (args,option1);       // initialize args

    do {
        cout << ++count << ". " << option << "\n";
    } while ((option = va_arg (args,char*)) != 0)

    va_end (args);                 // clean up args
    cout << "option? ";
    cin >> choice;
    return (choice > 0 && choice <= count) ? choice : 0;
} /* Menu */
```

To access the arguments, args is declared to be of type va_list and is initialized by calling va_start. The second argument to va_start must be the last function parameter explicitly declared in the function header (i.e., option1 here). Subsequent arguments are retrieved by calling va_arg. The second argument to va_arg must be the *expected* type of that argument (i.e., char* here).

For this technique to work, the last argument must be a 0, marking the end of the argument list. Va_arg is called repeatedly until this 0 is reached. Finally va_end is called to restore the runtime stack (which may have been modified by the earlier macros). The sample call

```
int choice = Menu("Open","Close","Revert","Delete","Quit",0);
```

will produce the following output

```
1. Open
2. Close
3. Revert
4. Delete
5. Quit
option?
```

Function members of a class can also take a variable number of arguments. Recall the LinEqns class (Section 6.5). We can define an additional constructor for this class that, rather than accepting a solution vector, takes the solution directly as arguments.

```
class LinEqns : public Matrix {
      int  nEqns;
      double* solution;
public:
      LinEqns (int n,double soln ...);        // additional constructor
      //...
};

LinEqns::LinEqns (int n,double soln ...) : Matrix(n,n+1)
{
      nEqns = n;
      solution = new double[n];
      va_list args;
      va_start(args,soln);

      solution[0] = soln;
      for (int i = 1; i < n; ++i)
          solution[i] = va_arg(args,double);
      va_end(args);
} /* LinEqns */
```

In this case, because any of the trailing arguments can be zero, we pass the exact number of arguments (excluding n) as the first argument.

EXERCISE 9.1   *solution provided*

Write a simplified version of `printf`:

```
void PrintF (char* ...);
```

It should scan its first argument, looking for format specifications of the form `%d`, `%f`, and `%s`, and output the subsequent arguments after casting them to the appropriate type. Note that no trailing 0 is necessary, since the number of arguments can be deduced from the number of format specifications in the first argument.

EXERCISE 9.2   *solution provided*

Rewrite `Menu` so that it associates each option with an action (denoted by a function pointer). For example, given the call.

```
Menu("Open",&Open,"Close",&Close,"Revert",0,"Quit",0,0);
```

`Menu` should call `Close` if the user chooses the `Close` option. Assume that all such functions are of type `void (*)(void)`. Pass 0 for options that have no associated action.

9.4 Generic classes

A class such as `Set` (Section 1.4) becomes really useful when it is independent of the type of elements a set may contain: the same class may be used to produce sets of integers, reals, strings, etc. Such classes are said to be **generic**.

C++ has no built-in facility to support the definition of generic classes, as Ada [Watt *et al.* 1987] for example does. However, other techniques can be used to simulate generic classes. The AT&T C++, for example, offers a header file named `generic.h` which contains some macros for defining generic classes by macro substitution. This method is quite cumbersome and only suitable for small classes, since the entire class has to be written as a macro.

The GNU C++ offers a more practical method, also based on text substitution, but handled by a separate tool (see Lea[1989] for a complete description). Here, a generic class is written by inserting type parameters in appropriate places. A concrete class may then be generated by running the tool and specifying concrete types to be substituted for the type parameters. The advantage of this approach is that generic classes have the appearance of normal classes, not macros.

C++ is still evolving and the future inclusion of a proper generic class definition facility is a possibility.

9.5 Files

Like C, C++ has no built-in facilities for I/O; instead, these are provided as libraries. They include the conventional I/O library of C (as denoted by the header file stdio.h) and further abstractions built on top of them. Except for input and output streams (see below) these abstractions are nonstandard and vary across implementations. The examples included in this chapter are based on the I/O libraries of GNU C++.

In C, a file is managed by a data structure (of type FILE) which records certain details of the file, and a set of functions for manipulating the file: opening, closing, reading, writing, etc. In C++, this is more conveniently expressed as a class.

```
class File {
      enum Mode {rMode,wMode,rwMode};
      FILE* filePtr;                 // file structure pointer
      char* fileName;                // file name
      Mode  mode;                    // read/write mode
      //...
public:
            File (char* name,char* mode)
            ~File ();
      File& open (char* name,char* mode);
      File& close ();
      File& get (char& ch);
      File& put (char ch);
      File& putback (char ch);
      //...
};
```

Most function members of File are defined in terms of their C counterparts.

A more commonly used abstraction is the notion of streams. There are two standard stream classes: ostream for output and istream for input. These are declared in the header file stream.h.

9.6 Streams

Ostream includes the output facilities of File together with a set of function members which overload the << operator for the output of objects of built-in types.

```
class ostream : File {
    //...
public:
    ostream& operator << (char);
    ostream& operator << (int);
    ostream& operator << (long);
    ostream& operator << (float);
    ostream& operator << (double);
    ostream& operator << (char*);
    //...
};
```

Two streams of type ostream are predefined in C++; cout denotes the default output stream and cerr denotes the default error stream.

Since operator<< returns a reference to ostream, multiple output statements can be combined into one.

```
cout << i << "\n";        // equivalent to: cout << i; cout << "\n";
```

The order of application is always left to right; << is first applied to cout and i, returning cout as the result which then becomes the left operand of the second <<.

```
(cout << i) << "\n";
```

This simple and uniform treatment of output for built-in types is easily extended to user-defined types by further overloading the << operator. For any given user-defined type T, we can define an operator<< function which outputs objects of type T.

```
ostream& operator << (ostream&,T&);
```

The first parameter must be a reference to ostream so that multiple uses of << can be grouped into one statement. The second parameter need not be a reference, but this is more efficient for large objects.

To give an example, recall the Set class (Sections 1.4 and 4.3). Instead of the function member Print, we can define an operator<< function and make it a friend of Set.

```
class Set {
    //...
    friend ostream& operator << (ostream&,Set&);
};
```

```
ostream& operator << (ostream& out,Set& s)
{
    out << "{";
    for (int i = 0; i < s.card-1; ++i)
        out << s.elems[i] << ",";
    if (s.card > 0)
        out << s.elems[s.card-1];
    out << "}";
    return out;
} /* operator << */
```

Given this definition, << can be used for the output of sets in a manner identical to its use for the built-in types. For example, assuming that s1 and s2 denote the sets {10,20,30} and {10,30,50}, respectively, the statement

```
cout << s1 << " + " << s1 << " = " << s1+s2 << "\n";
```

will produce the following output:

```
{10,20,30} + {10,30,50} = {10,20,30,50}
```

In addition to its simplicity and elegance, this style of output eliminates the burden of remembering the name of the output function for each user-defined type, and enables us to write compound output statements that involve many different (built-in or user-defined) types. For example, without the use of overloaded <<, the last example would have to written as (assuming that \n has been removed from Print):

```
s1.Print();      cout << " + ";      s2.Print();
cout << " = ";   (s1 + s2).Print();
```

Formatted output in ostream is facilitated by a function member named form. This function is called in exactly the same way as printf in C; it formats its arguments and returns a string result. Hence, it can be used with the << operator

```
cerr << form("index %d is out of range in %s\n",idx,name);
```

where %d and %s are the usual format specifications for decimals and strings, respectively. Form cannot be used directly for the formatted output of user-defined type objects.

The input stream class istream includes the input facilities of File together with a set of function members which overload the >> operator for the input of objects of built-in types.

```
class istream : File {
    //...
public:
    istream& operator >> (char&);
    istream& operator >> (int&);
    istream& operator >> (long&);
    istream& operator >> (float&);
    istream& operator >> (double&);
    istream& operator >> (char*);
    //...
};
```

C++ provides a predefined stream of type istream, named cin, which denotes the default input stream.

The parameters of the function members of istream are declared as references since they are altered by the functions. As before, because operator>> returns a reference to istream, multiple input statements can be combined into one.

```
cin >> i >> s;                  // equivalent to: cin >> i; cin >> s;
```

Input of user-defined types is facilitated by further overloading the >> operator. Referring back to the Set class, we can overload operator>> for reading sets expressed in the mathematical notation {...}.

```
istream& operator >> (istream& in, Set& s)
{
    int elem;
    char ch = ' ';
    Bool comma = false;

    s.card = 0;             // initially s should be empty
    in >> ch;
    if (ch == '{')
        for (;;) {
            in >> ch;
            switch (ch) {
                case '}': if (comma)
                              in.clear(_bad);           // corrupt
                          return in;
```

```
                    case ',': if (comma || s.card == 0) {
                                  in.clear(_bad);              // corrupt
                                  return in;
                              }
                              comma = true;
                              break;
                    case ' ':                                 // ignore blanks
                    case '\t':
                    case '\r': break;
                    default:  in.putback(ch);                 // undo: in >> ch;
                              in >> elem;
                              if (!in.good() || s.card > 0 && !comma) {
                                  in.clear(_bad);              // corrupt
                                  return in;
                              }
                              s.AddElem(elem);
                              comma = false;
                              break;
            } /* switch */
        } /* while */
    return in;
} /* operator >> */
```

This function performs some error checking to ensure that the input syntax is correct. If not, it calls the `clear` function to set the state of the input stream to _bad.[2] Also, after reading a set element, it calls `good` to ascertain the validity of the read number. The function returns the input stream as soon as it reads the final } or when it detects an error.

EXERCISE 9.3

Use the set input and output operators to define `SetCalc`, a function which reads a set expression that may contain set operators, evaluates it, and prints the result. Assume that the input is terminated by a period. The following examples illustrate typical inputs:

```
{5,6,7}.
{3,4} + {4,6,3}.
{5,6,3} * {6,55,4,3} + {5,8} + {}.
```

---

[2] Refer to the C++ I/O library manual of your system for a description of these functions.

9.7 Summary

Read-only variables and function parameters should be declared as **constants**. For a pointer, one can declare the pointer itself, or the object pointed to, or both to be constant. Constants and **enumerations** can be local to classes.

A **structure** is a class all of whose members are public. Structures and classes can be **nested** as a notational convenience, but always remain global.

A function whose last parameter is followed by ellipses (. . .) may take a **variable number of arguments**. These arguments are processed by a set of macros defined in stdarg.h.

C++ has no built-in facility for defining **generic** classes. These can be simulated using macros or other forms of text substitution.

Input and output is usually performed using **streams**. The class ostream overloads << for the output of built-in types. The class istream overloads >> for the input of built-in types. The user may further overload << and >> for the input and output of user-defined types.

CHAPTER 10

Case Study: B-trees

This chapter looks at the implementation of B-trees as a case study. After a brief introduction, a B-tree class is presented. We then look at some variations of B-trees and show how a variation can be implemented as a derived class. The latter clearly illustrates single inheritance and the use of virtual functions.

10.1 Introduction

The information stored on a secondary storage device, such as a hard disk, can be organized in a variety of ways. On-line systems which manipulate huge quantities of data require efficient representations that enable rapid searching for a data item. Indexed files are usually used for this purpose.

An indexed file consists of a set of **records**, where each record contains a unique **key** and some **data**. As a minimum, the following operations should be provided for an indexed file:

Search: given a key, find the data associated with the key.
Insert: add a new record to the file.
Delete: given a key, remove the record having that key.

B-trees [Comer 1979] represent one of the most efficient ways of implementing an indexed file. A B-tree consists of a set of nodes, where each node may contain up to 2n records and have 2n+1 children. The number n is called the **order** of the tree. Every node in the tree (except for the root node) must have at least n records. This ensures that at least 50% of the storage capacity is utilized. Furthermore, a nonleaf node that contains m records must have exactly m+1 children.

Figure 10.1 shows a B-tree of order 2. For clarity, only the key value of each record is displayed. Assuming an ascending order, all keys in a node appear in increasing order from left to right, and for any given key k, the keys in the left subtree of k are less than k and the keys in the right subtree of k are greater than k.

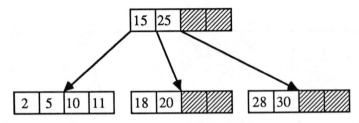

Figure 10.1 A B-tree of order 2.

The data associated with a key can either appear in the node, next to the key, or be stored separately by just storing its address (a pointer) in the node. The latter approach is more flexible since it can support variable-length records.

The most important property of a B-tree is that the insert and delete operations are designed so that the tree remains balanced at all times. In general, a balanced tree has a smaller height than an unbalanced tree. This can significantly reduce the search time.

To insert a record into a B-tree, one simply starts from the root node, searching downward for the node into which the record should be inserted. After finding the node, the record is inserted in the node so that it remains sorted. For example, inserting a record whose key is 19 in the above tree will produce the tree shown in Figure 10.2.

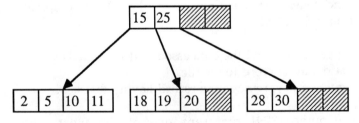

Figure 10.2 The tree after key 19 has been inserted.

There is, however, no guarantee that the node into which we intend to insert is not already full. For example, if we try to insert the key value 1 into the above tree, we will confront a full node. In this case, the full node is split into two nodes of equal size and the middle key is passed up to the parent node (see Figure 10.3).

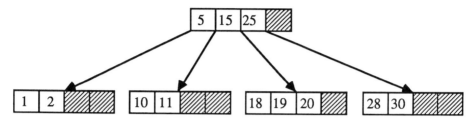

Figure 10.3 The tree after key 1 has been inserted.

Of course, the parent node may be full too, in which case it is also split. The splitting process may propagate in this fashion all the way to the root node. Since the root node has no parent, splitting it will produce 3 nodes, leaving only one key in the new root (see Figure 10.4).

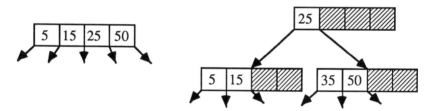

Figure 10.4 Inserting 35 into a full root (left) causes it to split into 3 nodes (right).

To delete a record from a B-tree, we start from the root node and search downward for the node containing its key. If the required node is a leaf node, we simply remove the key from the node. For example, deleting 19 from Figure 10.2 takes us back to Figure 10.1.

However, if the required node is a nonleaf node then we must find an adjacent key to fill the vacant position so that the tree remains balanced. To find an adjacent key, we search for the left-most key (k) in the left-most leaf in the right subtree (r) of the deleted key. By definition, every key in r is greater than k. Hence moving k into the vacant position will keep the tree balanced and valid. For example, deleting 15 from Figure 10.2 will cause 18 to be moved in its position (see Figure 10.5).

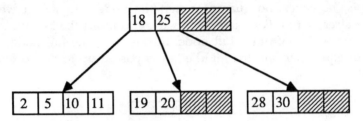

Figure 10.5 Deleting 15 from the tree in Figure 10.2.

A delete operation, therefore, always propagates to a leaf node, causing a key to be removed from it. However, there might not be enough keys in the leaf node to warrant a deletion. If the leaf node contains exactly n key (n being the order of the tree) then the deletion will violate the definition of a B-tree (i.e., cause an *underflow*). The solution is to borrow a key from a neighboring leaf, or even better, to evenly *distribute* the contents of the leaf node and its neighbor between them. For example, deleting 19 from Figure 10.5 will cause an underflow. So the remaining key in this node, the contents of its left neighbor, and the parent key are evenly distributed between them (see Figure 10.6).

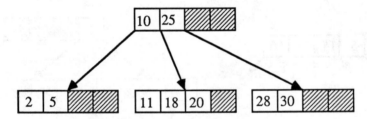

Figure 10.6 Deleting 19 from Figure 10.5.

A further complication is for a neighbor of an underflown leaf to contain exactly n keys, in which case we cannot borrow from it. This is resolved by merging the two leaf nodes to produce a single leaf node, and inserting the parent key inside it. For example, deleting 28 from Figure 10.1 will cause a merge of this kind (see Figure 10.7).

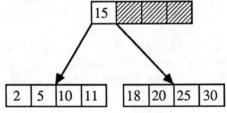

Figure 10.7 Deleting 28 from Figure 10.1.

Of course, this may also cause an underflow in the parent node, requiring the same procedure to be applied to that node (i.e., distribution or merging). The process may propagate all the way to the root node. However, remember that, unlike other nodes, the root node is allowed to remain underflown. It gets merged with another node only when it becomes empty.

Searching a B-tree is straightforward. A search for a key k always starts from the root node and works its way downwards. When searching a node, we look for an exact match for k, and failing that, we look for two keys $k1$ and $k2$ so that $k1 < k < k2$, and then move on to the right subtree of $k1$. However, if $k2$ is the left-most key in the node, we move on to the left-most subtree of the node. Similarly, if $k1$ is the right-most key of the node, we move on to the right-most subtree of the node. The process continues until the key is found.

Efficient implementation of B-trees requires fast disk access operations. To improve performance, typically the size of a node is set to be equal to a disk page (block) so that accessing a node becomes a single I/O operation. Each page also contains a *modify* flag. When a node is accessed, its page is read into main memory and its flag is set to false. While the page is in memory, if we make a change to it, the flag is set to true. When we have no further use for the page, its flag is checked: if it is true then the page is written back to the disk; otherwise, it is simply discarded.

In the discussions that follow, we will use an in-core representation of B-trees. Although this may have little use in practice, it has the advantage of clarifying the way the operations work. Converting this to a more realistic implementation requires a little extra work, namely, implementing the pointers as disk addresses and mapping nodes to disk pages.

10.2 A B-tree class

First of all, we need some way of representing nodes and records in a B-tree. For simplicity, let us assume that a record (see Item below) consists of an integer key, a real data part, and a pointer to its right subtree.

Each node in the tree (see Page below) consists of a count of the number of items in the node, a pointer to the left-most subtree of the node, and a set of items. Note that items is defined as an array of 1 element so that its actual size can be determined later, when allocating storage for a Page (see NewPage).

The BTree class consists of a pointer to the root of the tree, a buffer space to be used for distribution and merging of nodes, an indication of the order of the tree, and a set of function members, 6 of which are public.

Below, each function member is described separately, with its code appearing, so far as possible, on the same page as the description.

```
#include <stream.h>
#include <ctype.h>
enum Bool { false, true };
typedef int Key;
typedef double Data;

struct Page;
struct Item {
    Key    key;                      // item's key
    Data   data;                     // item's data
    Page*  right;                    // pointer to right subtree
};
struct Page {
    int    size;                     // no. of items on the page
    Page*  left;                     // pointer to the left-most subtree
    Item   items[1];                 // the items on the page (dynamic)
};
class BTree {
protected:
    const maxOrder = 256;            // max tree order
    Page*  root;                     // pointer to root node
    Item*  buf;                      // buffer for distribution and merging
    int    order;                    // order of tree
    Page*  NewPage      ();
    void   FreePage     (Page* page);
    Bool   SearchAux    (Page* tree,Key key,Item* item);
    Bool   BinarySearch (Page* node,Key key,int* idx);
    Item*  InsertAux    (Item* item,Page* node);
    void   DeleteAux1   (Key key,Page* node,Bool* underflow);
    void   DeleteAux2   (Page* parent,Page* node,int idx,Bool* underflow);
    void   Underflow    (Page* node,Page* child,int idx,Bool* underflow);
    int    CopyItems    (Item* src,Item* dest,int count);
    int    InsertItem   (Item* item,Item* items,int idx,int size);
    int    DeleteItem   (Item* items,int idx,int size);
    void   PrintAux     (Page* node,int margin);
public:
           BTree        (int order);
           ~BTree       ()                      {FreePage(root);}
    Bool   Search       (Key key,Item* item)
                                        {return SearchAux(root,key,item);}
    void   Insert       (Key key,Data data);
    void   Delete       (Key key);
    void   Print        (int margin = 0)   {PrintAux(root,margin);}
};
```

BTree::BTree (int order)

The constructor checks that the requested `order` is a valid one, initializes `root`, and allocates space for `buf`. When the requested order is less than 1 or greater than `maxOrder`, `order` is set to 1 (i.e., a 3-way tree).

BTree::~BTree ()
void BTree::FreePage (Page* page)

The destructor is defined inline and simply call `FreePage`. The latter takes a pointer to a page as argument and recursively frees the storage occupied by the node and all its subtrees.

inline Page* BTree::NewPage ()

This function allocates storage for a new page. It uses `order` to determine the dimension of the `items` array in a page.

```
BTree::BTree (int order)
{
    if (order < 1 || order > maxOrder)
        order = 1;
    root = 0;
    BTree::order = order;
    buf = new Item[2*order + 2];
} /* BTree */

void
BTree::FreePage (Page* page)
{
    if (page != 0) {
        FreePage (page->left);
        for (int i = 0; i < page->size; ++i)
            FreePage (page->items[i].right);
        delete page;
    }
} /* FreePage */

inline Page*
BTree::NewPage ()
{
    return (Page*) new char[sizeof(Page) + order*2*sizeof(Item) - 1];
} /* NewPage */
```

Bool BTree::Search (Key key,Item* item)
Bool BTree::SearchAux (Page* tree,Key key,Item* item)
Bool BTree::BinarySearch (Page* node,Key key,int* idx)

Search searches for an item whose key is equal to key and returns a pointer to that item in item. Search is defined inline and simply calls SearchAux, which does the actual work by recursively searching the tree. The latter searches a node by calling BinarySearch. BinarySearch searches for key amongst the keys in node, returning true if it finds the key, and false otherwise. It also returns, in idx, the position of the key in the node if it finds it, or the expected position of the key, if it does not find it.

```
Bool
BTree::SearchAux (Page* tree,Key key,Item* item)
{
    int idx;
    if (tree == 0)
        return false;
    if (BinarySearch(tree,key,&idx)) {
        *item = tree->items[idx];
        return true;
    }
    return SearchAux((idx < 0 ? tree->left
                               : tree->items[idx].right),key,item);
} /* SearchAux */

Bool
BTree::BinarySearch (Page* node,Key key,int* idx)
{
    int  low = 0;
    int  up = node->size - 1;
    int  mid;
    Bool found;
    do {                                       // binary chop
        mid = (low + up) / 2;
        if (key <= node->items[mid].key)
            up = mid - 1;                      // restrict to lower half
        if (key >= node->items[mid].key)
            low = mid + 1;                     // restrict to upper half
    } while (low <= up);
    *idx = (found = low - up > 1) ? mid : up;
    return found;
} /* BinarySearch */
```

void BTree::Insert (Key key,Data data)
Item* BTree::InsertAux (Item* item,Page* node)
Insert inserts a record item into the tree, with the given key and data. When the
tree is empty, this is done by creating a new page and inserting the item in that
page. Otherwise the insertion is done by calling InsertAux.

InsertAux first searches the current node by calling BinarySearch. If the key is
already in the node then it simply returns 0. Otherwise, it uses the idx returned
by BinarySearch to determine the next subtree to move on to. If the subtree is not
empty, then InsertAux is called recursively for that subtree. Otherwise, the node
is a leaf node, and the item is inserted immediately by calling InsertItem,
provided the node is not full.

A full node is split by creating a new node, copying the contents of the full
node into buf, inserting the item into buf, and then distributing the contents of
buf (except for the middle item) between the old node and the new node. The
middle item in buf is then returned to the caller of InsertAux, and becomes the
parent of the two nodes. The new node always becomes the right neighbor of the
old node. The left-most subtree of the new node (denoted by p0) is set to the right
subtree of the middle item, ensuring that the tree remains balanced.

```
void
BTree::Insert (Key key,Data data)
{
    Item* receive, item;
    Page* page;
    item.key = key;
    item.data = data;
    item.right = 0;
    if (root == 0) {                            // empty tree
        root = NewPage();
        root->left = 0;
        root->items[0] = item;
        root->size = 1;
    } else if ((receive = InsertAux(&item,root)) != 0) {
        page = NewPage();                       // new root
        page->size = 1;
        page->left = root;
        page->items[0] = *receive;
        root = page;
    }
} /* Insert */
```

```
Item*
BTree::InsertAux (Item* item, Page* node)
{
    Page *child, *page;
    int  idx, size, half;
    if (BinarySearch(node, item->key, &idx))
        return 0;                           // already in tree
    if ((child = idx < 0 ? node->left : node->items[idx].right) != 0)
        item = InsertAux(item, child);      // child is not a leaf
    if (item != 0) {                        // node is a leaf, or passed up
        if (node->size < 2*order)           // insert in the node
            node->size = InsertItem(item, node->items, idx+1, node->size);
        else {                              // node is full, split
            page = NewPage();
            size = CopyItems(node->items, buf, node->size);
            size = InsertItem(item, buf, idx+1, size);
            node->size = CopyItems(buf, node->items, half = size/2);
            page->size = CopyItems(buf+half+1, page->items, size-half-1);
            page->left = buf[half].right;
            *item = buf[half];              // the mid item
            item->right = page;
            return item;
        }
    }
    return 0;
} /* InsertAux */


void
BTree::Delete (Key key)
{
    Bool underflow;
    Page* temp;
    DeleteAux1(key, root, &underflow);
    if (underflow && root->size == 0) {     // dispose root
        temp = root;
        root = root->left;
        delete temp;
    }
} /* Delete */
```

void BTree::Delete (Key key)
void BTree::DeleteAux1 (Key key,Page* node,Bool* underflow)
Delete deletes a record item having the key key. It calls DeleteAux1 to do the
deletion and then checks for underflow. An underflow, in this case, would be an
indication of deleting the last item in the root node, in which case the root is set
to its left-most subtree and its node is deleted.

DeleteAux1 deletes an item whose key is equal to key from the subtree
denoted by node. It returns true in underflow if this causes an underflow, and false
otherwise. DeleteAux1 first searches the current node by calling BinarySearch. If
the key is already in the node then it deletes the item by calling DeleteItem,
provided the node is a leaf. Otherwise, it calls DeleteAux2 to do the deletion, and
if this causes an underflow, calls Underflow to handle it.

When the required item is not in the current node, DeleteAux1 uses idx to
determine the next subtree to be searched, and calls itself recursively for that
subtree. Also in this case, a check is made for an underflow and handled by
calling Underflow.

```
void
BTree::DeleteAux1 (Key key,Page* node,Bool* underflow)
{
    Page* child;
    int   idx;
    *underflow = false;
    if (node == 0) return;
    if (BinarySearch(node,key,&idx)) {
        if ((child=(idx - 1 < 0 ? node->left
                                : node->items[idx-1].right)) == 0) {
                                                    // node is a leaf
            node->size = DeleteItem(node->items,idx,node->size);
            *underflow = node->size < order;
        } else {                                    // node is a subtree
            DeleteAux2(node,child,idx,underflow);   // delete from subtree
            if (*underflow)
                Underflow(node,child,idx-1,underflow);
        }
    } else {                                        // is not in this node
        child = (idx < 0 ? node->left : node->items[idx].right);
        DeleteAux1(key,child,underflow);            // should be in child
        if (*underflow)
            Underflow(node,child,idx,underflow);
    }
} /* DeleteAux1 */
```

void BTree::DeleteAux2 (Page* parent,Page* node,int idx,Bool* underflow)
void BTree::Underflow (Page* node,Page* child,int idx,Bool* underflow)
DeleteAux2 deletes the item denoted by idx from parent. Node denotes a subtree of parent from which an item may be borrowed to fill the vacant position.

First, child is set to the right-most subtree of node. If this is nonempty then node is nonleaf, in which case DeleteAux2 is called recursively to go a further level down the subtree. A check is made for an underflow after the recursive call, and handled by calling Underflow. At some stage during these recursive calls, a leaf node is finally reached (when child becomes 0). An item is borrowed from the leaf node by copying it into the vacant position in parent and deleting it from node by calling DeleteItem. Note the way the right subtree of the vacant position is preserved by storing it in the temporary variable right and then setting it for the borrowed item.

Underflow handles all underflows and is called when the number of items in a node becomes less than order. Child is the underflown node, node is the parent node of child, and idx denotes the parent item in node, one of whose subtrees (left or right) is child. Underflow repairs the underflown node by either borrowing items from a neighboring node, or by merging it with a neighboring node.

```
void
BTree::DeleteAux2 (Page* parent,Page* node,int idx,Bool* underflow)
{
    Page* child = node->items [node->size-1] .right;
    Page* right;
    if (child != 0) {                               // node is not a leaf
        DeleteAux2 (parent,child,idx,underflow);  // go another level down
        if (*underflow)
            Underflow (node,child,node->size-1,underflow) ;
    } else {                                        // node is a leaf
        right = parent->items [idx] .right;
        // borrow an item from node for parent:
        parent->items [idx] = node->items [node->size-1];
        parent->items [idx] .right = right;
        node->size = DeleteItem (node->items,node->size-1,node->size) ;
        *underflow = node->size < order;
    }
} /* DeleteAux2 */
```

First, two pointers, left and right, are set to the left and right subtrees of the parent item. Then the contents of left node, the parent item, and the contents of right node are copied into buf. If the resulting size is larger than the maximum size of a node, the contents of buf are evenly distributed between left and right, and the middle item is placed in node, taking the place of the parent item. Otherwise, left and right are merged into left, and right is deleted. In this case, the parent item is also deleted from node, since it now resides in left.

   In general, a merge may cause further underflows. However, this will not cause Underflow to call itself recursively. Instead, true is returned in the underflow parameter; it is the responsibility of the caller of Underflow to check this.

```
void
BTree::Underflow (Page* node,Page* child,int idx,Bool* underflow)
{
    Page* left = (idx < node->size-1
                    ? child : (idx == 0
                                ? node->left : node->items[idx-1].right));
    Page* right = (left == child ? node->items[++idx].right : child);
    int  size, half;
    // copy contents of left, parent item, and right into buf:
    size = CopyItems (left->items,buf, left->size);
    buf[size] = node->items[idx];
    buf[size++].right = right->left;
    size += CopyItems (right->items,buf+size,right->size);
    if (size > 2*order) {            // distribute buf between left and right
        left->size = CopyItems (buf, left->items,half = size/2);
        right->size = CopyItems (buf+half+1,right->items,size-half-1);
        right->left = buf[half].right;
        node->items[idx] = buf[half];
        node->items[idx].right = right;
        *underflow = false;
    } else {                         // merge, and free the right page
        left->size = CopyItems (buf, left->items,size);
        node->size = DeleteItem (node->items,idx,node->size);
        delete right;
        *underflow = node->size < order;
    }
} /* Underflow */
```

int BTree::CopyItems (Item* src, Item* dest, int count)
int BTree::InsertItem (Item* item, Item* items, int idx, int size)
int BTree::DeleteItem (Item* items, int idx, int size)
CopyItems copies count items from src to dest and returns count as its result.
InsertItem inserts item into items at a position denoted by idx. Size denotes the
original number of items. InsertItem returns size+1 as its result. DeleteItem
deletes the item denoted by idx from items. Size denotes the original number of
items. DeleteItem returns size-1 as its result.

void BTree::Print (int margin = 0)
void BTree::PrintAux (Page* node, int margin)
Print prints a tree. This is defined inline and simply calls PrintAux to do the
actual printing. PrintAux prints a tree or subtree denoted by node. Margin is a left
margin for printing the items in a node. PrintAux first prints the left-most
subtree of a node by calling itself recursively for that subtree and then uses a loop
to print each item in the node together with its right subtree. The result is a tree
hanging from the left of the screen to the right.

```
int
BTree::CopyItems (Item* src, Item* dest, int count)
{
    for (int i = 0; i < count; ++i)          // straight copy
        dest[i] = src[i];
    return count;
} /* CopyItems */


int
BTree::InsertItem (Item* item, Item* items, int idx, int size)
{
    for (int i = size; i > idx; --i)         // shift right
        items[i] = items[i-1];
    items[idx] = *item;                      // insert
    return size + 1;
} /* InsertItem */


int
BTree::DeleteItem (Item* items, int idx, int size)
{
    for (int i = idx; i < size-1; ++i)       // shift left
        items[i] = items[i+1];
    return size - 1;
} /* DeleteItem */
```

```
void
BTree::PrintAux (Page* node, int margin)
{
    char margBuf[128];
    if (node != 0) {
        for (int i = 0; i <= margin; ++i)        // build the margin string
            margBuf[i] = ' ';
        margBuf[i] = 0;
        PrintAux(node->left, margin+8);          // print the left-most child
        for (i = 0; i < node->size; ++i) {
            cout << form("%s(%3d,%.2f)\n",        // print an item
                    margBuf, node->items[i].key, node->items[i].data);
            PrintAux(node->items[i].right, margin+8);  // print right child
        }
    }
} /* PrintAux */

main ()
{
    Key  key, key1, key2;
    char option[20];
    Item item;
    BTree tree(2);                               // B-tree of order 2
    for (;;) {
        cout << "S)earch, I)nsert, D)elete, P)rint, Q)uit ? ";
        cin >> option;
        if (isupper(*option)) *option = tolower(*option);
        switch (*option) {
            case 's':  cout << "key? ";    cin >> key;
                       if (tree.Search(key, &item))
                           cout << "data = " << item.data << "\n";
                       else
                           cout << "no such item.\n";
                       break;
            case 'i':  cout << "key = from, to? ";  cin >> key1 >> key2;
                       for (key = key1; key <= key2; ++key)
                           tree.Insert(key, key+0.5);
                       break;
            case 'd':  cout << "key? ";    cin >> key;
                       tree.Delete(key);   break;
            case 'p':  tree.Print();       break;
            case 'q':  exit(0);
        } /* switch */
    } /* for */
} /* main */
```

The `main` function is a simple user interface for testing the B-tree class. To enable rapid insertion of many items at once, the program allows the user to specify a range of keys, and for each key k, it sets the data field of the item to $k+0.5$. A sample run of the program is shown below.

```
S)earch, I)nsert, D)elete, P)rint, Q)uit ? i
key = from, to? 10 22
S)earch, I)nsert, D)elete, P)rint, Q)uit ? p
            ( 10,10.50)
            ( 11,11.50)
      ( 12,12.50)
            ( 13,13.50)
            ( 14,14.50)
      ( 15,15.50)
            ( 16,16.50)
            ( 17,17.50)
      ( 18,18.50)
            ( 19,19.50)
            ( 20,20.50)
            ( 21,21.50)
            ( 22,22.50)
S)earch, I)nsert, D)elete, P)rint, Q)uit ? d
key? 14
S)earch, I)nsert, D)elete, P)rint, Q)uit ? p
            ( 10,10.50)
            ( 11,11.50)
      ( 12,12.50)
            ( 13,13.50)
            ( 15,15.50)
            ( 16,16.50)
            ( 17,17.50)
      ( 18,18.50)
            ( 19,19.50)
            ( 20,20.50)
            ( 21,21.50)
            ( 22,22.50)
S)earch, I)nsert, D)elete, P)rint, Q)uit ? s
key? 19
data = 19.5
S)earch, I)nsert, D)elete, P)rint, Q)uit ? q
$
```

10.3 B*-trees

A B*-tree is a B-tree in which most nodes are at least 2/3 full (instead of 1/2 full). Instead of splitting a node as soon as it becomes full, an attempt is made to evenly distribute the contents of the node and its neighbor(s) between them. A node is split only when one or both of its neighbors are full too. A B*-tree facilitates more economic utilization of the available store, since it ensures that at least 66% of the storage occupied by the tree is actually used. As a result, the height of the tree is smaller, which in turn improves the search speed.

The search and delete operations are exactly as in a B-tree; only the insertion operation is different. Consider the following B*-tree, and suppose that we want to insert key 3.

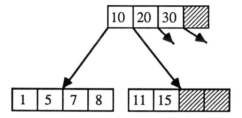

Figure 10.8 A B*-tree.

Key 3 should obviously be inserted in the left child; however, this child is full. Instead of splitting the child (as in a B-tree) we examine its right neighbor (or the left neighbor if there is no right neighbor). The right neighbor is not full, so we evenly distribute the contents of the left child, the right child, key 3, and the parent key (i.e., 10) between the three of them (see Figure 10.9).

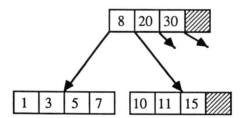

Figure 10.9 The tree after inserting key 3.

Of course, there is no guarantee that a neighboring node will have empty slots; it may be full too (see Figure 10.10).

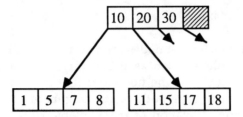

Figure 10.10 A node and its neighbor are full.

In this case the two full nodes are split into 3 and the keys are distributed between the 3 nodes as evenly as possible (see Figure 10.11).

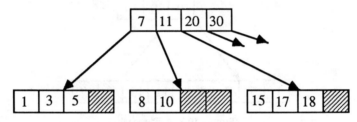

Figure 10.11 Splitting 2 full nodes into 3.

In both cases, we say that an *overflow* has occurred. Of course, the parent node may be already full too, in which case the overflow is propagated up, and if necessary, all the way to the root node. However, when the root node overflows, it is split into 3 nodes, as in a B-tree (see Figure 10.4).

10.4 A B*-tree class

Since a B*-tree shares much with a B-tree (i.e., same internal representation and identical search and delete operations), the most natural way of defining it is as a derived class of BTree. Let us call the derived class BStar. We should redefine the function members which perform the insert operation. To do so, we declare Insert and InsertAux as virtual in the base class. The only new member to be included in the derived class is Overflow; this is positioned in the private part of BStar.

```
class BTree {                                      // base class
protected:
    //...
    virtual Item* InsertAux (Item* item,Page* node);
public:
    //...
    virtual void  Insert    (Key key,Data data);
};

class BStar : public BTree {                       // derived class
    Item* InsertAux (Item* item,Page* node);
    Item* Overflow  (Item* item,Page* node,Page* child,int idx);
public:
    void  Insert    (Key key,Data data);
};

void
BStar::Insert (Key key,Data data)
{
    Item* overflow, item;
    Page *left, *right;
    Bool dummy;
    item.key = key;
    item.data = data;
    item.right = 0;
    if (root == 0) {                          // empty tree
        root = NewPage();
        root->left = 0;
        root->items[0] = item;
        root->size = 1;
    } else if ((overflow = InsertAux(&item,root)) != 0) {
        left = root;                          // root becomes a left child
        root = NewPage();
        right = NewPage();
        root->left = left;                    // the left-most child of root
        root->items[0] = *overflow;           // the overflown item
        root->items[0].right = right;         // the right child of root
        root->size = 1;
        right->left = overflow->right;
        right->size = 0;
        Underflow(root,right,0,&dummy);       // right is underflown: size 0
    }
} /* Insert */
```

void BStar::Insert (Key key, Data data)
Item* BStar::InsertAux (Item* item, Page* node)
The new version of `Insert` deals with root overflows by splitting the root into 3 nodes. It creates a new root, moves the overflow item to the new root, makes the old root the left child of the new root, and creates an empty node as the right child of the new root. Since the right child is now empty (i.e., underflown), the `Underflow` function is called to make the necessary rearrangements.

`InsertAux` searches the current node, as before, and return 0 if the key is already in the node. Unlike before, after inserting the item into a nonleaf node, it calls `Overflow` if the recursive call to `InsertAux` returns an overflown item. Also, to insert into a full leaf, instead of splitting the leaf, it inserts the item (using `buf`) and then returns the overflown item. The caller of `InsertAux` (either `Insert` or `InsertAux` itself) will then deal with the overflow.

```
Item*
BStar::InsertAux (Item* item, Page* node)
{
    Page* child;
    int  idx;
    if (BinarySearch(node, item->key, &idx))
        return 0;                                     // already in tree
    if ((child = idx < 0 ? node->left : node->items[idx].right) != 0) {
        if ((item = InsertAux(item, child)) != 0)     // child not a leaf
            return Overflow(item, node, child, idx);
    } else if (node->size < 2*order) {                // item fits in node
        node->size = InsertItem(item, node->items, idx+1, node->size);
    } else {                                          // node is full
        CopyItems(node->items, buf, node->size);
        InsertItem(item, buf, idx+1, node->size);
        CopyItems(buf, node->items, node->size);
        *item = buf[node->size];
        return item;
    }
    return 0;
} /* InsertAux */


Item*
BStar::Overflow (Item* item, Page* node, Page* child, int idx)
{
    Page* left = (idx < node->size-1
                    ? child : (idx == 0 ? node->left
                                        : node->items[idx-1].right));
    Page* right = (left == child ? node->items[++idx].right : child);
```

```
        Page* page;
        int  size, half, mid1, mid2;

        // copy left, overflown and parent items, and right into buf:
        size = CopyItems(left->items,buf,left->size);
        if (child == left ) {
            buf[size++] = *item;
            buf[size] = node->items[idx];
            buf[size++].right = right->left;
            size += CopyItems(right->items,buf+size,right->size);
        } else {
            buf[size] = node->items[idx];
            buf[size++].right = right->left;
            size += CopyItems(right->items,buf+size,right->size);
            buf[size++] = *item;
        }
        if (size < 4*order+2) {            // distribute buf between left and right
            left->size = CopyItems(buf,left->items,half = size/2);
            right->size = CopyItems(buf+half+1,right->items,size-half-1);
            right->left = buf[half].right;
            node->items[idx] = buf[half];
            node->items[idx].right = right;
            return 0;
        } else {                          // split int 3 pages
            page = NewPage();
            mid1 = left->size = CopyItems(buf,left->items, (4*order+1)/3);
            mid2 = right->size = CopyItems(buf+mid1+1,right->items,4*order/3);
            mid2 += mid1+1;
            page->size = CopyItems(buf+mid2+1,page->items, (4*order+2)/3);
            right->left = buf[mid1].right;
            buf[mid1].right = right;
            page->left = buf[mid2].right;
            buf[mid2].right = page;
            node->items[idx] = buf[mid2];
            if (node->size < 2*order) {
                node->size = InsertItem(&buf[mid1],node->items,idx,node->size);
                return 0;
            } else {
                *item = node->items[node->size-1];
                InsertItem(&buf[mid1],node->items,idx,node->size-1);
                return item;
            }
        }
    }
} /* Overflow */
```

Item* BStar::Overflow (Item* item, Page* node, Page* child, int idx)

Item is the overflown item and child is the overflown node, whose parent item is denoted by idx in node. As in Underflow, left and right are set to the left and right subtrees of the parent item.

Overflow first copies the contents of left, the overflown item, the parent item, and the contents of right into buf. If the total number of items in buf is less than 4*order+2 then the contents of buf is evenly distributed between left and right, and the middle item replaces the parent item. Otherwise, a new node is created and the contents of buf are evenly distributed between left, right, and the new node. The second remaining item replaces the parent item, and the first remaining item is inserted in node. The latter may cause an overflow, in which case the overflown item is returned to the caller of Overflow.

The B*-tree program can be tested using the same driver, by simply changing the definition of tree in main to:

```
    BStar tree(2);                    // B*-tree of order 2
```

Running the B*-tree program using the same test data clearly shows that it does delay the splitting of nodes.

```
    S)earch, I)nsert, D)elete, P)rint, Q)uit ? i
    key = from, to? 10 22
    S)earch, I)nsert, D)elete, P)rint, Q)uit ? p
                ( 10,10.50)
                ( 11,11.50)
                ( 12,12.50)
        ( 13,13.50)
                ( 14,14.50)
                ( 15,15.50)
                ( 16,16.50)
                ( 17,17.50)
        ( 18,18.50)
                ( 19,19.50)
                ( 20,20.50)
                ( 21,21.50)
                ( 22,22.50)
    S)earch, I)nsert, D)elete, P)rint, Q)uit ? q
    $
```

EXERCISE 10.1

Run the B-tree and the B*-tree programs, inserting keys 1-200 in a tree of order 2. Compare the number of visited nodes in either case for finding a key in a leaf node.

10.5 B'-trees

A B'-tree is another variation of the B-tree in which all keys (and their associated data) are placed in the leaf nodes. The intermediate nodes are organized as a B-tree and serve as an **index** for the entire tree. An intermediate node contains only pseudo keys, the exact values of which are not really important, so long as they can guide a search to the correct leaf. The leaves of a B'-tree are usually linked together, to also facilitate sequential search. Figure 10.12 shows an example.

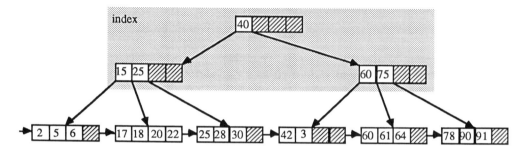

Figure 10.12 A B'-tree.

Searching is done as before, except that the search does not terminate when a key value is found, but progresses all the way to a leaf node. This is because some of the pseudo keys may be identical to the actual keys in the leaves.

During insertion, when a leaf node is split into two, a *copy* of the middle key is passed up, leaving the middle key in the right leaf. For example, consider inserting key 8 into the following tree.

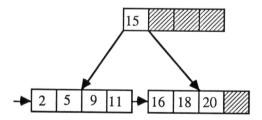

Figure 10.13 Left leaf is full.

The left leaf is split into two, leaving the middle key (i.e., 8) in the right leaf, and sending a copy of it to the parent node (see Figure 10.14).

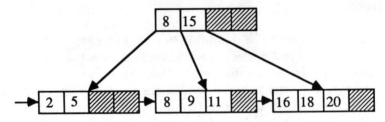

Figure 10.14 Key 8 inserted.

Deletion is somewhat easier, since it only concerns the keys in the leaves. No rearrangement is necessary, provided the leaf remains at least half full. Otherwise, the same distribution or merging process as in a B-tree should be applied.

The fundamental differences between B'-trees and B-trees suggest that the former cannot be conveniently defined as a derived class of the latter. (Note that, in general, the intermediate nodes and the leaves of a B'-tree may have different structures.) We present here only a sketch of the class, leaving its implementation as an exercise.

```
struct NodeItem {
     Key   key;
     void* right;
};

struct LeafItem {
     Key  key;
     Data data;
};

struct NodePage {
     PageKind kind;              // should be set to nodePage
     int       size;
     void*     left;
     NodeItem items[1];
};

struct LeafPage {
     PageKind  kind;             // should be set to leafPage
     int        size;
     LeafPage* next;             // pointer to next leaf
     LeafItem  items[1];
};
```

```
class BDash {
    enum PageKind {nodePage, leafPage};
    const maxOrder = 256;         // max tree order
    NodePage* root;               // random access
    LeafPage* seq;                // sequential access (left-most leaf)
    void* buf;
    int  order;
    //...
public:
    //...
};
```

Because there are two types of page, some of the pointers are declared to be of type `void*`. Explicit type casting should be used when dereferencing such pointers.

EXERCISE 10.2

Use the above declarations to implement the BDash class.

10.6 Summary

B-trees are a popular way of implementing indexed files on random access secondary storage devices. The insert and delete operations associated with a B-tree ensure that the tree is always balanced. By definition, a B-tree utilizes at least 50% of the occupied storage.

B*-tree is a variation of the basic B-tree. By delaying the splitting of nodes during insertion, it ensures that at least 66% of the occupied storage is utilized.

B'-tree is another variation of the basic B-tree. It consists of two type of nodes: nonleaf nodes which are organized as a B-tree and act as an index, and leaf nodes which contain the actual keys and are linked together to enable sequential access.

CHAPTER 11

Case Study: Memory Management

This chapter looks at the organization and management of the heap in high-level programming languages. The use of heap storage is first introduced, followed by a heap management program which controls the allocation and deallocation of blocks. The concept of pointers is then extended to *handles* to support the use of relocatable blocks. An implementation of the latter is presented as a derived class. Finally, some suggestions for improving the programs are presented.

11.1 Introduction

Modern imperative programming languages divide the memory space into at least two areas: the stack and the heap. These two grow in opposite directions (see Figure 11.1). The stack is used for holding the activation records of routines when they are called during execution. The heap is the source of storage space for dynamically created blocks (e.g., using new in C++). Since blocks may be created and destroyed in an arbitrary order, it is necessary to keep track of them.

Various algorithms have been developed to manage this task. Our discussion is centered around one such algorithm, called the **boundary tag method** [Horowitz and Sahni 1987]. In this method, the heap storage consists of two components: used blocks and free blocks. The latter are organized as a doubly-linked-list, called the **free list**. When a request for a new block is made, the free list is searched for a block large enough to grant the request. That block (or part thereof) is then allocated and removed from the list. When a block is freed, it is merged with neighboring free blocks (if any) and then added to the free list. By merging free blocks (when possible), the algorithm avoids the proliferation of small blocks in the free list.

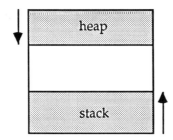

Figure 11.1 Stack and heap growth.

The structure of a block is shown in Figure 11.2. Each block carries two separate overheads: a header and a footer. The header contains pointers to the previous and the next block in the list, the size of the block (in bytes), and a tag which indicates whether the block is in use or free. The footer contains a pointer to the beginning of the block and a tag identical to the one in the header.

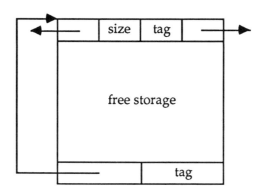

Figure 11.2 The structure of a block.

Originally, the entire storage is organized as a list of 2 blocks (see Figure 11.3). The first block is a dummy block and is included to simplify the management of the list. This is followed by a large block of the available storage, and a dummy header. The latter marks the end of the memory and simplifies the compaction algorithm (see Section 11.2). The dummy block and the final dummy header are permanently in use (tag = 1). The large block is initially free (tag = 0). The 3 components appear consecutively in physical memory, that is, the free block appears immediately after the dummy block and the dummy header appears immediately after the free block.

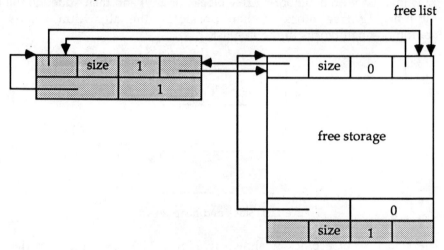

Figure 11.3 The initial organization of the free list.

After some processing there may be a number of free blocks in the free list. A request for a new block of size n is handled as follows. Starting from the block denoted by 'free list', we search for a block of size $\geq n$. If we arrive back at 'free list' during the search then we conclude that no such block exists and hence the request is rejected. Otherwise, the chosen block is used for allocation (see Figure 11.4).

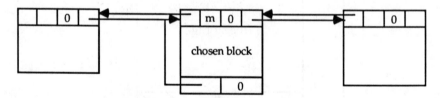

Figure 11.4 A fragment of the free list.

Assuming that the size of the block is m, two cases are possible. If $m-n \leq e$, where e is a small number, we allocate the entire block: the block is removed from the free list, its tags are set to 1, and a pointer to its free storage is returned (see Figure 11.5). Otherwise, n bytes are allocated from the bottom of the block, the size of the original block is reduced to $m-n$, and a pointer to the free storage of the allocated block is returned (see Figure 11.6). This ensures that the free list will never contain a block smaller than e, thereby improving the overall performance of the algorithm.

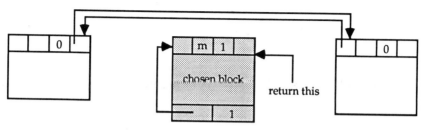

Figure 11.5 Allocating an entire block.

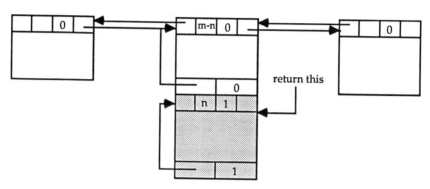

Figure 11.6 Allocating a portion of a block.

When a block of size n is freed, we examine its neighboring blocks (i.e., blocks that appear immediately above and below it in physical memory) to see if they are free too, in which case, they are merged with the block. Assume that the preceding and succeeding blocks are, respectively, of size p and q, four cases are possible.

If both neighboring blocks are in use then the freed block is simply inserted in the free list. If only the preceding block is free then its size is increased by n. If only the succeeding block is free then the size of the freed block is increased by q, and it is inserted in the place of the succeeding block in the free list. Finally, if both neighboring blocks are free then the size of the preceding block is increased by $n+q$ and the succeeding block is removed from the free list.

Headers, footers, and pointer arithmetic facilitate quick examination of neighboring blocks. For example, given that b is a pointer to a block's header, a pointer to the footer of the preceding block and a pointer to the header of the succeeding block would, respectively, be:

```
prec = (footer*)b - 1;
succ = (header*) ((char*)b + b->size);
```

11.2 A dynamic memory class

A dynamic memory based on the boundary tag method is conveniently defined as a class with operations for allocating/deallocating blocks, getting the size of a block, and changing the size of a block. For simplicity, we have represented the heap as an array (see heap in DynMem below).

The structure of the headers and footers is as described above, except that a header also contains a double-pointer named master. The significance of this will be described in the next section. Another addition is wordSize, which denotes the size of a word in bytes. This is used to ensure that blocks are allocated on word boundaries and is required to be at least the size of int. Epsilon denotes the minimum size of a block and is required to be at least minEpsilon. The latter should always be greater than the overheads of a block, i.e., size of Header and Footer put together.

Given a pointer to a block's contents, HeadOf returns a pointer to its header, and given a pointer to a block's header, FootOf returns a pointer to its footer. BlockOf does the reverse of HeadOf. PrevHead and NextHead return, respectively, pointers to the headers of the preceding and succeeding blocks.

InsertBlock inserts a block in freeList and sets its tag to vacant. RemoveBlock removes a block from freeList. Note that freeList is set to point to the left block before removing the block. This ensures that freeList will never end up pointing to a removed block!

The remaining member functions are individually described below.

```
struct Header {           // block header
        Header*  lLink;       // left link
        Header*  rLink;       // right link
        void**   master;      // master of this block
        int      size;        // size of block in bytes
        Status   tag;         // block status
};

struct Footer {           // block footer
        Header*  uLink;       // up link
        Status   tag;         // block status
};
```

```
class DynMem {
protected:
    const maxHeap = 16384;              // 16K bytes
    const minWordSize = sizeof(int);
    const minEpsilon = sizeof(Header) + sizeof(Footer) + 4;
    enum  Status { vacant, used };  // block status
    char    heap[maxHeap];              // heap storage
    int     wordSize;                   // word size
    int     epsilon;                    // a small number
    Header* freeList;
    Header* HeadOf    (void* block) {return (Header*)block-1;}
    Footer* FootOf    (Header* h)   {return (Footer*)((char*)h+h->size)-1;}
    void*   BlockOf   (Header* h)   {return (void*) (h + 1);}
    Header* PrevHead  (Header* h)   {return ((Footer*)h - 1)->uLink;}
    Header* NextHead  (Header* h)   {return (Header*)((char*)h + h->size);}
    void    InsertBlock (Header* h);
    void    RemoveBlock (Header* h);
public:
            DynMem    (int = minEpsilon, int = minWordSize);
    void*   NewPtr    (int bytes);
    void    FreePtr   (void* ptr);
    int     PtrSize   (void* ptr)
                {return HeadOf(ptr)->size - sizeof(Header) - sizeof(Footer);}
    void*   ResizePtr (void* ptr, int newSize);
};


inline void
DynMem::InsertBlock (Header* head)
{
    head->tag = FootOf(head)->tag = vacant;
    head->lLink = freeList;
    head->rLink = freeList->rLink;
    head->rLink->lLink = head->lLink->rLink = head;
} /* InsertBlock */


inline void
DynMem::RemoveBlock (Header* head)
{
    freeList = head->lLink;
    head->rLink->lLink = head->lLink;
    head->lLink->rLink = head->rLink;
} /* RemoveBlock */
```

DynMem::DynMem (int eps = minEpsilon, int wSize = minWordSize)
The constructor initializes `freeList` so that it corresponds to Figure 11.3. The
dummy block (denoted by `head1`) is positioned at the beginning of the heap and
the dummy header (denoted by `headN`) at the end of the heap. The space in
between is organized as one large free block (denoted by `blkHead`) to which
`freeList` points.

Both arguments of the constructor have default values. `DynMem` adjusts these
when they have unreasonable values.

```
DynMem::DynMem (int eps, int wSize)
{
    if (eps < minEpsilon)
        eps = minEpsilon;
    if (wSize < minWordSize)
        wSize = minWordSize;
    epsilon = eps;
    wordSize = wSize;
    Header* head1  = (Header*) heap;
    Footer* foot1  = (Footer*) (head1 + 1);
    Header* blkHead = (Header*) (foot1 + 1);
    Footer* blkFoot = (Footer*)
                      (heap + maxHeap - sizeof(Footer) - sizeof(Header));
    Header* headN  = (Header*) (blkFoot + 1);
    // initialise the 1st block's header and footer:
    head1->lLink = head1->rLink = blkHead;
    head1->tag = foot1->tag = used;
    head1->size = sizeof(Header) + sizeof(Footer);
    foot1->uLink = head1;
    // initialise the free block's header and footer:
    blkHead->lLink = blkHead->rLink = head1;
    blkHead->tag = blkFoot->tag = vacant;
    blkHead->size = maxHeap - sizeof(Header) * 2 - sizeof(Footer);
    blkFoot->uLink = blkHead;
    // initialise the last block's header (no footer):
    headN->lLink = headN->rLink = 0;
    headN->tag = used;
    headN->size = sizeof(Header);
    // freeList initially points to the first free block:
    freeList = blkHead;
} /* DynMem */
```

void* DynMem::NewPtr (int bytes)

NewPtr attempts to allocate a block containing at least bytes free bytes. It first increases bytes by the overheads of a block (i.e., a header and a footer) and then, if necessary, adjusts bytes so that it is a multiple of wordSize.

Starting from the block denoted by freeList, NewPtr searches for a free block of size ≥ bytes. It allocates the whole block if dividing it would result in a free block of size ≤ epsilon. Otherwise, it allocates from the bottom of the block, leaving the remaining portion in the free list. NewPtr returns a pointer to the contents of the allocated block, if successful, and 0 otherwise.

```
void*
DynMem::NewPtr (int bytes)
{
    Header* head;        // head of the block to be allocated
    Footer* foot;        // block's footer
    int     diff;
    if (bytes <= 0) return 0;
    bytes += sizeof(Header) + sizeof(Footer);     // for overheads
    if (bytes % wordSize != 0)               // if not multiple of wordsSize...
        bytes = (bytes/wordSize + 1) * wordSize;  // ...then align
    head = freeList->rLink;
    do {                                     // find a suitable block
        if (!(head->tag & used) && head->size >= bytes) {
            if ((diff = head->size - bytes) <= epsilon) {
                RemoveBlock(head);             // allocate whole block
                foot = FootOf(head);
            } else {                           // allocate from bottom
                head->size = diff;             // remaining free portion
                (foot = FootOf(head))->uLink = head;
                foot->tag = vacant;
                head = (Header*)(foot + 1);    // the allocated block
                head->size = bytes;
                (foot = FootOf(head))->uLink = head;
            }
            head->master = 0;                  // no master
            head->tag = foot->tag = used;
            return BlockOf(head);
        }
        head = head->rLink;
    } while (head != freeList->rLink);
    return 0;
} /* NewPtr */
```

void DynMem::FreePtr (void* ptr)

FreePtr takes a pointer to the contents of a block (i.e., one returned by NewPtr) and frees that block. It attempts to compact memory by merging the freed block with neighboring blocks if they happen to be free too (see Section 11.1).

The block is inserted in the free list only when both neighboring blocks are in use, or when the preceding block is in use and its succeeding block is free. In the latter case, the succeeding block is removed from the free list, since it becomes part of the freed block. When both neighboring blocks are free, the succeeding block is removed from the free list after the 3 blocks have been merged.

```
void
DynMem::FreePtr (void* ptr)
{
    Header* head = HeadOf(ptr);          // the block to be freed
    Footer* foot = FootOf(head);
    Header* prev = PrevHead(head);       // the top adjacent block
    Header* next = NextHead(head);       // the bottom adjacent block
    int     size = head->size;
    if ((prev->tag & used) && (next->tag & used)) {
        // both adjacent blocks are in use:
        InsertBlock(head);
    } else if (!(prev->tag & used) && (next->tag & used)) {
        // only the preceding block is free:
        prev->size += size;
        foot->tag = vacant;
        foot->uLink = prev;
    } else if ((prev->tag & used) && !(next->tag & used)) {
        // only the succeeding block is free:
        head->size += next->size;
        foot->uLink = head;
        RemoveBlock(next);
        InsertBlock(head);
    } else {
        // both adjacent blocks are free:
        prev->size += size + next->size;
        FootOf(prev)->uLink = prev;
        RemoveBlock(next);
    }
} /* FreePtr */
```

```
void*
DynMem::ResizePtr (void* ptr,int newSize)
{
    int size = PtrSize(ptr);
    int diff;
    Header* head = HeadOf(ptr);
    Footer* foot;
    if (newSize < 0 || newSize == size)
        return ptr;
    if (newSize < size) {                          // reduce size
        diff = size - newSize;
        if (diff > minEpsilon) {                   // break into 2 blocks
            head->size -= diff;
            (foot = FootOf(head))->uLink = head;
            foot->tag = head->tag;
            (head = NextHead(head))->size = diff;
            FootOf(head)->uLink = head;
            InsertBlock(head);
        }
        return ptr;
    } else {                                       // increase size
        diff = newSize - size;
        Header* prev = PrevHead(head);
        Header* next = NextHead(head);
        int prevSize = ((prev->tag & used) ? 0 : prev->size);
        int nextSize = ((next->tag & used) ? 0 : next->size);
        Status tag = head->tag;
        size = head->size;
        if (diff > prevSize + nextSize)
            return ptr;                            // can't increase
        if (prevSize > 0) {
            head = prev;
            RemoveBlock(prev);
        }
        if (nextSize > 0)
            RemoveBlock(next);
        head->size = size + prevSize + nextSize;
        (foot = FootOf(head))->uLink = head;
        head->tag = foot->tag = tag;
        return ResizePtr(BlockOf(head),newSize);   // in case it's too big
    }
} /* ResizePtr */
```

```
int   PtrSize  (void* ptr)
```
```
void* DynMem::ResizePtr (void* ptr,int newSize)
```
PtrSize is defined inline and returns the size of a block denoted by ptr. This is obtained by subtracting the size of the block overhead from its actual size.

ResizePtr attempts to change the size of a block denoted by ptr to newSize. If newSize is less than the block size then the block is divided into two parts, provided this does not produce a free block of size ≤ epsilon. The released portion is then inserted in the free list.

When newSize is greater than the block size, ResizePtr examines the neighboring blocks to see if they are free and large enough so that when merged with the block the resulting block is of size ≥ newSize. If so, the merging is performed and ResizePtr is recursively called for the resulting block, in which case, ResizePtr divides the block if necessary.

ResizePtr returns a pointer to the modified block, but does not guarantee that a block can be successfully enlarged, nor does it guarantee that the contents of the block remain unchanged. It is the responsibility of the caller of ResizePtr to check these.

```
DynMem d;
//...
void* p = d.NewPtr(20);
//...
p = d.ResizePtr(p,100);
if (d.PtrSize(p) >= 100)
    //...
```

11.3 Relocatable memory

Memory blocks described so far are nonrelocatable, that is, when allocated they cannot be moved around in memory, since this will invalidate the block pointer. The disadvantage of this approach is that random allocation and deallocation of blocks may leave the heap fragmented. This slows further processing and reduces the chance of finding a block large enough to grant a request. Relocatable blocks overcome this difficulty by using a **handle** rather than a pointer to refer to a block. A handle is a pointer to a master pointer which in turn points to a block (see Figure 11.7).

This form of double reference implies that a master pointer can be changed (to point to another block) without affecting the handle. As a result, blocks can be easily moved around in physical memory, for example, to transform a fragmented heap to one which consists of a consecutive set of used blocks and a remaining large, free block (see Figure 11.8).

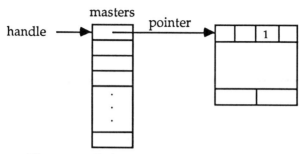

Figure 11.7 Referring to a block by a handle.

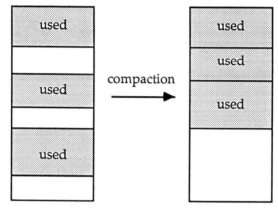

Figure 11.8 Memory compaction merges free blocks.

The master pointers are held in a central table and each allocated block contains a pointer to its master. This is why we included an additional field, master, in the Header structure (see previous section): when a block is relocated, master is used to update the master pointer in the table.

11.4 A relocatable memory class

The relocatable memory facility is easily defined as a derived class of DynMem. The required change is minor: Status is extended to include a new value (relocatable) for marking relocatable blocks.

The table of masters is allocated from the bottom of heap, and the new class contains a pointer to the beginning of the table, an indication of the size of the table, and an index, denoting the current master in the table. For relocation purposes, RelMem uses a private member function named MoveBlock which simply copies a block from one location to another.

```
#include <stream.h>

class RelMem : public DynMem {
    const minMasters = 16;              // min no. of masters
    enum { vacant, used, relocatable };
    void** masters;                     // master pointers
    int    nMasters;                    // number of masters
    int    masIdx;                      // current master index
    void   MoveBlock (Header* src, Header* dest);
public:
           RelMem    (int = minMasters, int = minEpsilon, int = minWordSize);
    void** NewHand    (int bytes);
    void   FreeHand   (void** hand)   { FreePtr(*hand); *hand = 0; }
    int    HandSize   (void** hand)   { return PtrSize(*hand); }
    void   ResizeHand (void** hand, int newSize);
    void   LockHand   (void** hand);
    void   UnlockHand (void** hand);
    int    Compact    ();
};


inline void
RelMem::MoveBlock (Header* src, Header* dest)
{
    register bytes = src->size;
    register char* from = (char*)src;
    register char* to = (char*)dest;

    while (bytes--)                     // copy bytes
        *to++ = *from++;
    FootOf(dest)->uLink = dest;
    *(dest->master) = BlockOf(dest);
} /* MoveBlock */
```

RelMem::RelMem (int nMas = minMasters,int eps = minEpsilon,
                        int wSize = minWordSize) : (eps,wSize)
The constructor takes an argument in addition to those taken by the constructor
for DynMem. Eps and wSize are directly passed to the latter. NMas, which denotes the
number of required masters, is required to be ≥ minMasters, but ≤ a quarter of the
size of the free block.

The free block is reduced in size to provide room for the table of master
pointers. This table is placed at the bottom of heap. All masters are initialized to 0,
as well as the master index masIdx.

void** RelMem::NewHand (int bytes)
This function allocates and returns a handle to a block of size bytes. The master
table is first searched for a vacant master pointer. The search starts at the position
denoted by masIdx and wraps around if necessary.

The block is allocated by calling NewPtr. If this fails, Compact is called which
compacts (see below) and returns the size of the largest free block. If this is large
enough, NewPtr is called again. Finally, the allocated block is marked as
relocatable, the address of its contents is stored in the acquired master, and the
address of the master is stored in the master field of the block and returned
immediately.

NewHand returns 0 when it fails to allocate a block of the requested size or
when the master table is full.

```
RelMem::RelMem (int nMas,int eps,int wSize) : (eps,wSize)
{
    Header* head = freeList;
    Footer* foot = FootOf(head);
    // adjust nMas if too small or too large:
    if (nMas < minMasters || nMas > (head->size - minEpsilon)/4)
        nMas = minMasters;
    nMasters = nMas;
    head->size -= nMasters * sizeof(void*);
    Footer* newFoot = FootOf(head);
    Header* newHead = (Header*) (newFoot + 1);
    head = (Header*) (foot + 1);
    *newFoot = *foot;
    *newHead = *head;
    masters = (void**) (newHead + 1);
    // initially all masters are free:
    for (register int i = 0; i < nMasters; ++i)
        masters[i] = 0;
    masIdx = 0;                       // the first free master
} /* RelMem */
```

```
void**
RelMem::NewHand (int bytes)
{
    register int i;
    void*    ptr;
    for (i = masIdx; i < nMasters && masters[i] != 0; ++i)
        ;                                           // find a master
    if (i >= nMasters) {
        for (i = 0; i < masIdx && masters[i] != 0; ++i)

            ;
        if (i >= masIdx)
            return 0;                               // run out of masters
    }
    masIdx = i;                                     // allocate master
    if ((ptr = NewPtr(bytes)) == 0)
        if (Compact() < bytes + sizeof(Header) + sizeof(Footer))
            return 0;                               // run out of heap
        else
            ptr = NewPtr(bytes);
    Header* head = HeadOf(ptr);
    head->tag = FootOf(head)->tag |= relocatable;
    masters[masIdx] = ptr;
    return (head->master = masters + masIdx);
} /* NewHand */


void
RelMem::ResizeHand (void** hand, int newSize)
{
    *hand = ResizePtr(*hand, newSize);
    if (PtrSize(*hand) >= newSize)                  // try resizing the pointer
        HeadOf(*hand)->master = hand;
    else if (HeadOf(*hand)->tag & relocatable) {
        void** newHand = NewHand(newSize);
        if (newHand == 0)
            return;                                 // failed
        FreeHand(hand);
        *hand = *newHand;
        *newHand = 0;
        HeadOf(*hand)->master = hand;
    }
} /* ResizeHand */
```

void RelMem::ResizeHand (void** hand, int newSize)

ResizeHand attempts to change the size of the block denoted by hand to newSize. It tries to do this by calling ResizePtr (which in turn examines the neighboring blocks when the size of the block needs to be increased). However, should this fail, it tries to relocate the block, provided the block is relocatable. To do this it simply calls NewHand (which will do a memory compaction if necessary), frees the old block, and substitutes the master pointer of the new block for the old block.

Note that, unlike ResizePtr, ResizeHand does not return a handle, since the value of the original handle is unchanged.

void RelMem::LockHand (void** hand)

void RelMem::UnlockHand (void** hand)

These two members lock and unlock a block denoted by hand, respectively. A block is locked by setting the relocatable bit in its tag to 0, and unlocked by setting the bit to 1. Locking a block may be necessary when dereferencing the handle. For example, in

```
void** hand = r.NewHand(20);
//...
LockHand(hand);
for (void* ptr = *hand; *ptr; ++ptr)
    //...
UnlockHand(hand);
```

the locking of hand ensures that should memory compaction take place within the for-loop (because of another call to NewHand, say) the block denoted by hand can not be relocated and hence ptr will remain valid.

```
void
RelMem::LockHand (void** hand)
{
    Header* head = HeadOf(*hand);
    head->tag = FootOf(head)->tag &= ~relocatable;
} /* LockHand */

void
RelMem::UnlockHand (void** hand)
{
    Header* head = HeadOf(*hand);
    head->tag = FootOf(head)->tag |= relocatable;
} /* UnlockHand */
```

int RelMem::Compact ()
This function compacts heap by moving the relocatable blocks, as far as possible,
to the top of heap. Compact first removes everything from the free list, except for
the dummy block. It then scans heap, looking for relocatable blocks.

```
int
RelMem::Compact ()
{
    freeList = (Header*)heap;                    // keep only the 1st block
    freeList->lLink = freeList->rLink = freeList;
    Header* src = NextHead(freeList);
    Header* dest = src;
    Header* lastHead = (Header*)masters - 1;
    Footer* foot;
    int     largest = 0;
    for (;;) {
        if (!(src->tag & used))                  // free block
            src = NextHead(src);
        else if (src->tag & relocatable) {   // relocatable used block
            if (src != dest) {                   // relocate
                Header* tmp = NextHead(src);
                MoveBlock(src,dest);
                src = tmp;
                dest = NextHead(dest);
            } else
                src = dest = NextHead(src);
        } else if (src != dest) {                // nonrelocatable used block
            dest->size = (char*)src - (char*)dest;
            (foot = FootOf(dest))->uLink = dest;
            dest->tag = foot->tag = vacant;
            InsertBlock(dest);
            if (dest->size > largest)
                largest = dest->size;
            src = dest = NextHead(src);
        } else                                   // there is no gap
            src = dest = NextHead(src);
        if (src > lastHead)
            break;
    }
    return largest;
} /* Compact */
```

Having found a relocatable block, Compact checks if there is a gap between that block and the used block preceding it. If so, it moves the block up to close the gap. If during scanning, we reach a nonrelocatable block, the free block preceding it (if any) is added to the free list.

Scanning is facilitated by two variables: src and dest. Dest points to the beginning of the most recent free block, if any. Otherwise, it is the same as src. Src points to the current block being examined. Relocation takes place only when src ≠ dest. Figure 11.9 illustrates the way src and dest are used.

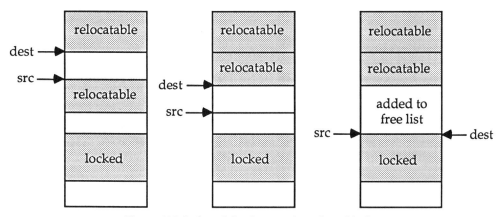

Figure 11.9 Left to right: the scanning of two blocks.

11.5 Improvements

There are a number of ways in which the algorithm can be improved. The first improvement involves the way the heap is represented. For this we used a fixed array. In practice, a more elaborate representation should be used. This may involve using the facilities of the host operating system to gain access to low-level memory management routines. When a request for a block fails, two courses of action are possible: either increase the size of the heap or do a memory compaction. A strategy which always tries the latter before the former, minimizes the growth of the heap. A strategy which does the opposite, compacts memory only when the heap reaches its maximum size. A trade-off between these two would be the most rational approach, discouraging the heap from getting too large by compacting it every now and then.

Another candidate for improvement is the table of master pointers. This, too, should be of variable size. For example, we can maintain the table as a linked-list of nonrelocatable blocks, adding a block to the list when we run out of master pointers, and removing a block from the list when all masters in that block are released. Such blocks may be allocated from the same heap or a separate one.

The way compaction is performed can be improved, too. In general, when a request fails, it is not necessary to compact the entire heap. For a large heap, this may be too expensive. It is often more economic to compact enough memory to release a block of the required size (or a multiple thereof). This can be done by a local compaction algorithm which, for example, looks at only a few blocks around a given block, but increases the compaction range until enough bytes have been released.

Since compaction requires the moving of entire blocks, the main bottleneck of the algorithm is MoveBlock. Things can be speeded up considerably by calling an operating system routine to do this, or, if no such routine is available, by coding MoveBlock in assembler.

EXERCISE 11.1

Rewrite the RelMem class so that the table of master pointers is organized as a doubly-linked-list of blocks. The masters pointer in the class should point to one of the blocks in this list. Initially, there should be only one such block, but as soon as we run out of masters, a new block should be allocated and added to the list. All such blocks must be nonrelocatable. Compact should check each such block to see if it is unused (i.e., all the masters equal to 0), in which case, it should free that block.

EXERCISE 11.2

As Figure 11.9 illustrates, as soon as Compact reaches a nonrelocatable block, it adds the preceding free block (if any) to the free list. Modify Compact so that it continues moving relocatable blocks to a free block even when such a condition arises, but adds the block to the free list when it is not large enough to accommodate the next relocatable block. This has the advantage of producing fewer, but larger, free blocks.

EXERCISE 11.3

Write a new member function, Merge, which merges two relocatable blocks to produce a larger block.

```
void** RelMem::Merge (void** hand1,void** hand2)
```

Merge should release one of the master pointers and use the other for the new block. It should check if the blocks are neighbors and do the merging in place. Otherwise, it should relocate one or both blocks as appropriate.

11.6 Summary

A **memory manager** is a program that controls the allocation and deallocation of memory blocks. Memory managers are typically used to control the organization of the **heap** storage.

One popular memory management algorithm is the **boundary tag method**. It maintains the available memory as a doubly-linked-list of blocks, where each block carries a header and a footer for housekeeping purposes.

A **handle** is a pointer to a pointer. The latter is called a master pointer and can be changed without affecting the former.

Use of handles instead of pointers for referring to blocks facilitates the relocation of blocks during memory compaction. Memory **compaction** transforms a fragmented heap into one which contains fewer but larger free blocks.

CHAPTER 12

Case Study: User Interface Manager

This case study describes the development of a User Interface Manager (UIM) which consists of four separate classes. The aim of the study is twofold: to produce a package that simplifies the development of user interfaces by offering useful facilities such as overlapping windows and menus, and to illustrate how the object-oriented style of C++ is used for such purposes. After a brief introduction, each class is described in detail. This is followed by an example showing how the package is used in an application program.

12.1 Introduction

A UIM is a piece of software that controls the communication between an application program and its end-user. It enables the user to provide input to the application and control the presentation of output. For most systems, the quality of the user interface determines the success of the system as a whole. However, good user interfaces are by no means easy to develop, and is some cases can account for up to 60% of the application code [Sutton and Sprague 1978]. Given the high development cost of user interfaces, any tool capable of reducing the effort can be valuable. This is where a UIM can be useful [Green 1985].

The main aim of a UIM is to simplify the development of a user interface by offering facilities that would otherwise have to be developed from scratch. To use these facilities, the application programmer simply calls the relevant functions offered by the UIM to do the required job. As far as the programmer is concerned, no knowledge of how each function works is necessary, only what each function does. Another advantage of a UIM is that it enables the designer to separate the user interface from the application logic. This is encouraged by modern design practices [Olsen 1983], since it simplifies the task of modifying a user interface and providing multiple interfaces to the same application.

Most modern user interfaces use a bitmap display as the output medium and mouse and keyboard as the input mediums. Unlike these, the UIM described in this chapter is aimed at commonplace terminals that consist of a CRT display and a keyboard. The current version of the package is based on a VT100 terminal, but can be easily adapted to other terminals. The terminal screen is viewed as a flat plane with two axes: columns increase from left to right and rows increase from top to bottom (see Figure 12.1).

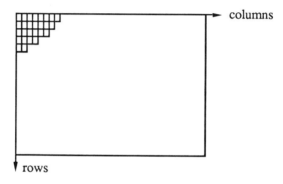

Figure 12.1 The terminal screen.

For separate compilation purposes, the package is broken down into a number of header and source files, as listed below.

FILE	CONTENTS
Common.h	global declarations included in all other header files
Terminal.h	declaration of the Terminal class
Window.h	declaration of the Window class
Menu.h	declaration of the Menu class
Form.h	declaration of the Form class
Global.cc	global variables and functions
Terminal.cc	implementation of the Terminal class
Window.cc	implementation of the Window class
Menu.cc	implementation of the Menu class
Form.cc	implementation of the Form class

12.2 Global declarations and definitions

The declarations in Common.h are used by all classes. PosCode writes to buf the code for positioning the cursor at a given location. WriteCode writes a string to standard output. The extern variables in Common.h are defined in Globals.cc (see below). Command is an enumeration of nonalphanumeric characters which are treated as commands. Mode is an enumeration of different (pen) printing modes. A character is represented by two bytes: the lower byte denotes the character code and the higher byte denotes its printing mode; these are retrieved, respectively, by charMask and modeMask. WindFlags is an enumeration of the values that can be stored in the flags field of a window; this is an integer whose lower byte denotes the window kind (i.e., plain, menu, form, or user defined). The hidden bit (in the higher byte) is set if the window is currently hidden. ErrKind denotes potential types of errors that may occur. A Point on the screen is represented by its row and column coordinates. Similarly, a Rectangle is represented by the coordinates of its sides.

Note the use of #ifndef macro in Common.h. This avoids the file being textually included more than once, no matter how many times it is included in another file. The same technique is used for other header files.

```
                              Common.h
#ifndef _COMMON_
#define _COMMON_
#include <ctype.h>
#include <std.h>
#define PosCode(buf,r,c)      sprintf(buf,posCode,r,c)
#define WriteCode(code)       write(1,code,strlen(code))
#define maxRows      23       // max no. of rows on the screen
#define maxCols      80       // max no. of columns on the screen
#define maxFlds      64       // max no. of fields in a form
#define maxLits      64       // max no. of literals in a form
#define bufSize     512       // buffer size
#define escape     '\033'     // escape character

extern char *posCode, *alfaCode, *graphCode, *plainCode, *revsCode,
            *defCode, *initCode, *clearCode, *bellCode;
extern char botRight, topRight, topLeft, botLeft, horizontal, vertical;
enum Bool    { false, true };
enum Command {           // keyboard commands
    escCmd    = -1,          // escape command
    upCmd     = -2,          // up arrow
    downCmd   = -3,          // down arrow
    leftCmd   = -4,          // left arrow
    rightCmd  = -5           // right arrow
};
```

```
enum Mode {              // pen mode
    defPen    = 0x0000,    // default pen
    graphPen  = 0x0100,    // graphic pen
    revsPen   = 0x0200,    // reverse video pen
    charMask  = 0x00FF,    // character mask
    modeMask  = 0xFF00     // pen mode mask
};
enum WindFlags {         // window flags
    plainWind = 0x0000,    // plain window
    menuWind  = 0x0001,    // menu window
    formWind  = 0x0002,    // form window
    user1     = 0x0004,    // user-defined window
    user2     = 0x0008,
    user3     = 0x0010,
    user4     = 0x0020,
    hidden    = 0x0100,    // invisible window
    kindMask  = 0x00FF     // window kind mask
};
enum ErrKind {           // error kind
    memErr, termErr, sysErr // memory, terminal, system error
};
struct Point {
    int row, col;
    Point  ()                { row = col = 0; }
    Point  (int r, int c)    { row = r;   col = c; }
    Offset (int r, int c)    { row += r; col += c; }
};

struct Rect {            // rectangle
    int top, left, bot, right;
        Rect         ()    { top = left = bot = right = 0; }
        Rect         (int top, int left, int bot, int right);
    void Offset      (int rows, int cols);
    Bool Empty       ()    { return left > right || top > bot; }
    Rect operator *  (Rect& rect);
    Rect operator +  (Rect& rect);
};
typedef void (*ErrFun) (int, const char*);
typedef void (*InterruptFun) (void);
class Terminal;
class Window;
class Menu;
class Form;
#endif _COMMON_
```

The string variables appearing at the beginning of `Global.cc` are used for controlling the terminal. The codes used here are for a VT100 terminal. To adapt the package to other terminals these may need to be changed. Each code is a sequence of bytes which when written to standard output will change some setting of the terminal. For example, `revsCode` causes subsequent printing to be done in reverse video, and `clearCode` clears the terminal screen.

The graphic characters are used for drawing the borders of a window. `TopRight`, for example, denotes the shape ¬. These characters are available only when the graphic character set is loaded (i.e., after `graphCode` has been written to standard output).

`Offset` offsets a `rect` by rows and cols. `Empty` returns true if and only if a rectangle is empty. `Operator*` finds the intersection of two rectangles: the rectangular area at which they overlap. `Operator+` calculates the union of two rectangles: the smallest rectangle that encloses both rectangles.

The `Interrupt` routine is called when a ^C interrupt occurs. It resets the terminal to its original mode and aborts the program with exit code 1.

Globals.cc

```
#include "Common.h"

// terminal control codes:
char* posCode   = "\033[%d;%dH";     // position cursor
char* alfaCode  = "\017";            // normal chars
char* graphCode = "\016";            // graphic chars
char* plainCode = "\033[0m";         // plain video
char* revsCode  = "\033[7m";         // reverse video
char* defCode   = "\017\033[0m";     // default: normal+plain
char* initCode  = "\033(B\033)0";    // initialize
char* clearCode = "\033[2J";         // clear screen
char* bellCode  = "\07";             // margin bell

// graphic characters:
char botRight   = '\152';
char topRight   = '\153';
char topLeft    = '\154';
char botLeft    = '\155';
char horizontal = '\161';
char vertical   = '\170';
```

```
Rect::Rect (int top,int left,int bot,int right)
{
    Rect::top = top;    Rect::left = left;
    Rect::bot = bot;    Rect::right = right;
} /* Rect */
void
Rect::Offset (int rows,int cols)
{
    top += rows;    left += cols;
    bot += rows;    right += cols;
} /* Offset */

Rect
Rect::operator * (Rect& rect)
{
    return Rect (top > rect.top ? top : rect.top,
          left > rect.left ? left : rect.left,
          bot < rect.bot ? bot : rect.bot,
          right < rect.right ? right : rect.right);
} /* operator * */

Rect
Rect::operator + (Rect& rect)
{
    return Rect (top < rect.top ? top : rect.top,
          left < rect.left ? left : rect.left,
          bot > rect.bot ? bot : rect.bot,
          right > rect.right ? right : rect.right);
} /* operator + */

#include "Term.h"

void
Interrupt ()
{
    Terminal::term->DefaultPen();
    ioctl(0,TIOCSETP,(char*) &(Terminal::ttym));
    exit(1);
} /* Interrupt */
```

12.3 The Terminal class

For clarity, the various attributes stored about a terminal are grouped within a class. An application program will require exactly one instance of this class; for this reason all private data members of this class are static. Ttym is a structure of type sgttyb (declared in the UNIX header file sgttyb.h). It records the current I/O mode of the terminal. ErrFun is a user-defined error function and is called when an error occurs. Rows and cols denote the dimensions of the terminal screen.

Screen is a dynamically allocated array of size rows*cols and is used for recording the contents of each individual character position on the screen. Region is an array of exactly the same dimensions as screen, each of whose elements is a pointer to the window which owns the character to which that element corresponds. Since windows can overlap, region is used to determine what area of any given window is visible at any time. Term is a pointer to an instance of the Terminal class. This static variable is used to access the function members of Terminal when no access to the class instance is available.

Windows are maintained in a linked-list. BotWind denotes the first window in the list (i.e., the one appearing behind all others). TopWind denotes the last window in the list (i.e., the top-most window). CurWind denotes the currently active window; this can be any window in the list. TermBuf is a private buffer for I/O purposes, e.g., preparing data to be written to the screen. CopyCode is a private function member for copying terminal codes to a buffer; after copying, it returns the address of the next vacant position in the buffer.

The first eight public function members in Terminal do not access the private part of the class and could have been defined outside the class. Their inclusion, however, is appropriate since they manipulate the physical terminal.

SetErrFun and GetErrFun are used, respectively, for setting and retrieving errFun. Using this pair, the programmer can save the current error function in a temporary variable, set it to another function and later on restore the original function. BotWind, TopWind, and CurWind simply return pointers to the corresponding windows in the window list. The remaining function members are described below in detail.

_____Terminal.h_____

```
#ifndef _TERM_
#define _TERM_
#include "Common.h"
#include <sys/ioctl.h>
#include <sgtty.h>
#include <signal.h>
```

```
class Terminal {
    static  sgttyb     ttym;                // original tty mode
    static  ErrFun     errFun;              // user error function
    static  int        rows, cols;          // screen size
    static  int*       screen;              // terminal screen
    static  Window**   region;              // window regions
    static  Terminal*  term;                // self reference
    static  Window*    botWind;             // bot window
    static  Window*    topWind;             // top window
    static  Window*    curWind;             // current window
    static  char       termBuf[bufSize];    // screen buffer
    char*   CopyCode   (char* buf, const char* code)
                       {strcpy(buf,code); return buf + strlen(code);}
public:
    void      AlfaPen     ()                 { WriteCode(alfaCode); }
    void      GraphPen    ()                 { WriteCode(graphCode); }
    void      PlainPen    ()                 { WriteCode(plainCode); }
    void      RevsPen     ()                 { WriteCode(revsCode); }
    void      DefaultPen  ()                 { WriteCode(defCode); }
    void      InitChars   ()                 { WriteCode(initCode); }
    void      Clear       ()                 { WriteCode(clearCode); }
    void      Bell        ()                 { WriteCode(bellCode); }
    void      SetErrFun   (ErrFun   ef)      { errFun = ef; }
    void      GetErrFun   (ErrFun* ef)       { *ef = errFun; }
    Window*   BotWind     ()                 { return botWind; }
    Window*   TopWind     ()                 { return topWind; }
    Window*   CurWind     ()                 { return curWind; }
              Terminal    (int rows = maxRows, int cols = maxCols);
              ~Terminal   ();
    void      Refresh     (Rect& rect, Window* from = 0);
    void      PenPos      (int row, int col);
    int       GetKey      ();
    void      Error       (ErrKind err, const char* msg);
    void      Message     (const char* msg);
    friend  void  Interrupt();
    friend  class Window;
    friend  class Menu;
    friend  class Form;
};
#endif _TERM_
```

Terminal::Terminal (int rows = maxRows, int cols = maxCols)
By checking the value of `term`, the constructor ensures that it is called only once.
Recall that `term` is a static member (initialized to 0 by default). Since the
constructor sets `term` to the `this` pointer (a nonzero value), it should be 0 at this
stage. Otherwise, `Error` is called.

The constructor arguments specify the dimensions of the screen. These are
checked to be within the permissible range. Otherwise `maxRows` and `maxCols` are
assumed. Next, storage for `screen` and `region` are allocated and all elements of
`region` are initialized to 0 (a 0 means that the corresponding character belongs to
no window).

_____Terminal.cc_____

```
#include "Term.h"
#include "Wind.h"


Terminal::Terminal (int rows, int cols)
{
    typedef void* VoidPtr;
    if (term != 0)                              // make sure called only once
        Error(termErr,"in Terminal");
    term = this;                                // self-reference
    Terminal::rows = rows = (rows <= 0 || rows > maxRows ? maxRows : rows);
    Terminal::cols = cols = (cols <= 0 || cols > maxCols ? maxCols : cols);
    if ((screen = new int[rows * cols]) == 0)
        Error(memErr,"for screen");
    if ((region = (Window**) new VoidPtr[rows * cols]) == 0)
        Error(memErr,"for region");

    // region should be initially blank:
    for (register row = 0; row < rows; ++row) {
        Window** rgn = region + cols * row;
        for (register col = 0; col < cols; ++col)
            *(rgn + col) = 0;
    }
    if (ioctl(0,TIOCGETP,(char*)&ttym) == -1)// get current mode
        Error(sysErr,"for ioctl");
    sgttyb tmp = ttym;                          // make a copy
    tmp.sg_flags |= CBREAK;                     // use cbreak mode
    tmp.sg_flags &= ~ECHO;                      // use no echo mode
    if (ioctl(0,TIOCSETP,(char*)&tmp) == -1)    // set the new mode
        Error(sysErr,"for ioctl");
    if (signal(SIGINT,&Interrupt) == (SignalHandler)(-1))
        Error(sysErr,"for signal");
    Clear();   InitChars();
} /* Terminal */
```

The current I/O mode is obtained by calling ioctl (see the UNIX header file sys/ioctl.h) and is stored in ttym. A copy of this is made in tmp and changed to set the mode to CBREAK and no ECHO. CBREAK means that characters typed at the terminal are not buffered and are available to the program immediately. No ECHO suppresses the echoing of the typed characters on the screen. The new mode is set by calling ioctl again. The original copy is retained for future use to, for example, restore the original mode (see Interrupt in Section 12.2).

The call to signal (see the UNIX header file signal.h) nominates Interrupt as the function to be called when a ^C interrupt occurs. Finally Clear and InitChars are called which, respectively, clear the terminal screen and initialize the terminal character set.

Terminal::~Terminal ()

The destructor frees the storage occupied by screen and region, and restores the original I/O mode by calling ioctl. It also sets the pen mode to its default value by calling DefaultPen.

void Terminal::Refresh (Rect& rect,Window* from = 0)

Refresh refreshes the portion of the screen denoted by rect and, in doing so, only considers the windows denoted by from in the window list. Rect is checked to be nonempty. When from is 0 all windows in the window list are considered.

First, using two nested for-loops, rect is 'erased' by storing blank and 0, respectively, in the corresponding positions of screen and region. Next, each visible window in the list denoted by from is considered, and the portion of the window that intersects rect is stamped onto screen and region. Note that all such updating is done off the screen. The final result is copied onto the screen in one go.

The area denoted by rect is refreshed line by line. The data for a line is built up in buf (this includes the codes for moving the cursor to the beginning of the line and for changing the pen mode). For each character in the line, the mode byte is extracted, and when this mode is different from that of the preceding character, the mode is changed by writing its code to buf. Once a line is completed, it is written to the screen by calling write.

Despite its complicated appearance, Refresh is very efficient. It minimizes the amount of data that has to be written to the screen in order to refresh rect. The obvious use of Refresh is for updating the appearance of the screen, e.g., when a window is opened, closed, hidden, moved, or resized.

```
Terminal::~Terminal ()
{
    delete screen;
    delete region;
    if (ioctl(0,TIOCSETP,(char*)&ttym) == -1)  // restore original mode
        Error(sysErr,"for ioctl");
    DefaultPen();
} /* ~Terminal */


void
Terminal::Refresh (Rect& rect,Window* from)
{
    register row, col;
    int width;
    if (rect.Empty()) return;
    if (from == 0)
        from = botWind;
    width = rect.right - rect.left + 1;

    // make rect and its region blank:
    for (row = rect.top; row <= rect.bot; ++row) {
        int* scr = screen + row * cols + rect.left;
        Window** rgn = region + row * cols + rect.left;
        for (col = 0; col < width; ++col) {
            *scr++ = ' ';   *rgn++ = 0;
        }
    }


    // update the part of screen and region denoted by rect
    // for each visible window in the list denoted by from:

    for (Window* wind = from; wind != 0; wind = wind->next)
        if (!wind->Hidden()) {
            Rect box = rect * wind->bounds;
            if (!box.Empty()) {
                int boxWidth = box.right - box.left + 1;
                int windWidth = wind->bounds.right - wind->bounds.left + 1;
                int leftDiff = box.left - wind->bounds.left;

                for (row = box.top; row <= box.bot; ++row) {
                    int* src = wind->area +
                            (row - wind->bounds.top) * windWidth + leftDiff;
```

```
                    int* dest = screen + row * cols + box.left;
                    Window** rgn = region + row * cols + box.left;
                    for (col = 0; col < boxWidth; ++col) {
                        *dest++ = *src++;
                        *rgn++ = wind;
                    }
                }
            }
        }

    DefaultPen();
    Mode mode, oldMode = defPen;

    // use screen to refresh the area denoted by rect:
    for (row = rect.top; row <= rect.bot; ++row) {
        char* buf = termBuf;
        int* scr = screen + row * cols + rect.left;
        PosCode(buf,row + 1,rect.left + 1);
        buf += strlen(buf);

        for (col = 0; col < width; ++col) {
            mode = *scr & modeMask;
            if (mode != oldMode) {
                if (oldMode & graphPen) {
                    if (!(mode & graphPen))
                        buf = CopyCode(buf,alfaCode);
                } else if (mode & graphPen)
                    buf = CopyCode(buf,graphCode);
                if (oldMode & revsPen) {
                    if (!(mode & revsPen))
                    buf = CopyCode(buf,plainCode);
                } else if (mode & revsPen)
                    buf = CopyCode(buf,revsCode);
                oldMode = mode;
            }
            *buf++ = *scr++ & charMask;
        }
        write(1,termBuf,buf - termBuf);
    }
    DefaultPen();
} /* Refresh */
```

void Terminal::PenPos (int row, int col)
Positions the pen (cursor) at coordinates row and col. These are automatically adjusted when out of range.

int Terminal::GetKey ()
Reads and returns a key press. The escape key has a special meaning. If pressed on its own then it must be pressed twice, in which case escCmd is returned. Pressing the arrow keys on a VT100 terminal produces 3 characters, the first of which is also escape. (For example, pressing the upper arrow key produces the sequence <ESC>[A.) These are scanned and returned appropriately. Escape followed by any other character is rejected by calling Bell.

```
void
Terminal::PenPos (int row, int col)
{
    row = (row < 0 ? 0 : (row >= rows ? rows - 1 : row));
    col = (col < 0 ? 0 : (col >= cols ? cols - 1 : col));
    PosCode(termBuf, row+1, col+1);
    write(1, termBuf, strlen(termBuf));
} /* PenPos */

int
Terminal::GetKey ()
{
    char ch;
    for (;;) {
        read (0, &ch, 1);
        if (ch == escape) {
            read(0, &ch, 1);
            switch (ch) {
                case escape: return escCmd;
                case '[':    read(0, &ch, 1);
                             switch (ch) {
                                 case 'A': return upCmd;
                                 case 'B': return downCmd;
                                 case 'C': return rightCmd;
                                 case 'D': return leftCmd;
                             } /* switch */
            } /* switch */
            Bell();   continue;
        } /* if */
        return (int) ch;
    } /* for */
} /* GetKey */
```

void Terminal::Error (ErrKind err, const char* msg)
This function handles errors. If a user-defined error function exists then it is called immediately and the error code (err) and the error message (msg) are directly passed on to it. Otherwise, the error is simply printed and Interrupt is called to abort the program.

void Terminal::Message (const char* msg)
The bottom row on the terminal screen is reserved for displaying special messages. All such messages are printed in reverse video. Long messages that cannot fit on a line are truncated with trailing ellipses. Since this may cause the current position of the cursor to be changed, Resume (see the next section) is called to move the cursor back to its original position.

```
void
Terminal::Error (ErrKind err,const char* msg)
{
    if (errFun != 0)
        (*errFun) (err,msg);
    else {
        sprintf(termBuf,"Error: %d %s\n",err,msg);
        write(1,termBuf,strlen(termBuf));
        Interrupt();
    }
} /* Error */

void
Terminal::Message (const char* msg)
{
    Point pt;
    Mode   mode;
    int    lastRow = rows;
    curWind->GetPos(&pt);
    curWind->GetMode(&mode);
    PenPos(lastRow,0);   RevsPen();
    strncpy(termBuf,msg,cols);
    register len = strlen(msg);
    if (len > cols) {
        termBuf[len = cols] = '\0';
        while (len >= cols - 3) termBuf[--len] = '.';
    } else
        while (len < cols) termBuf[len++] = ' ';
    write(1,termBuf,len);   curWind->Resume();
} /* Message */
```

12.4 The Window class

The window class denotes objects that are represented as rectangular boxes on the
screen. A window is a self-contained entity; it has a border, contains text, and has
a set of attributes. Windows may overlap in any order without affecting their
contents. A window may also be hidden; this is useful for preparing a window
off the screen and displaying it instantly. As far as I/O operations are concerned, a
window can be treated as a stream which can be written to and read from.

Flags is a set of boolean flags denoting the type and status of the window.
Title is simply a string of characters and is displayed on top of the window.
Bounds denotes the rectangular boundary of the window; this is described in
global screen coordinates. It provides a window with a local coordinate system.
The latter is used by all window manipulation operations. For example, location
(0,0) in a window *w* always denotes the top-left corner of *w*, regardless of where
w appears on the screen.

Pos and mode denote, respectively, the current pen position and mode for a
window. Each window has its own pen position and mode. Activating a window
always causes these attributes to take effect. Area is a dynamically allocated array,
organized as a two-dimensional matrix representing the contents of the window.
Prev and next are, respectively, pointers to the window that appears immediately
behind this window and the window that appears immediately in front of it.
Either or both may be 0. WindBuf is a private buffer for window I/O operations.

The first 5 public members retrieve and set attributes of a window. Hidden
returns true if a window is currently invisible, and false otherwise. Previous and
Next return, respectively, the window behind and the window in front of a
window. The remaining members are described below in detail.

Window.h

```
#ifndef _WIND_
#define _WIND_
#include "Common.h"

class Window {
    WindFlags flags;                        // window flags
    char*     title;                        // window title
    Rect      bounds;                       // window bounds rectangle
    Point     pos;                          // pen position
    Mode      mode;                         // pen mode
    int*      area;                         // area covered by the window
    Window*   prev;                         // previous window pointer
    Window*   next;                         // next window pointer
    static    char windBuf[bufSize];        // window buffer
```

```
    void      SetArea       (int top,int left,int bot,int right);
    void      Resume        ();
    void      WriteBehind   (const char* str,int row,int col,int len);
public:
    void      GetBounds     (Rect* rect)     { *rect = bounds; }
    void      GetPos        (Point* pt)      { *pt = pos; }
    void      GetMode       (Mode* pm)       { *pm = mode; }
    void      GetKind       (WindFlags* kd) { *kd = flags & kindMask; }
    void      SetKind       (WindFlags kd)  { flags = flags & ~kindMask | kd; }
    Bool      Hidden        ()               { return flags & hidden; }
    Window* Previous        ()               { return prev; }
    Window* Next            ()               { return next; }
              Window        (const char* title,int top,int left,
                                             int bot,int right);
              Window        (const char* title,Rect& bounds);
              ~Window       ();
    void      PenMode       (Mode pm);
    void      PenPos        (int row,int col);
    void      Move          (int row,int col);
    void      Resize        (int top,int left,int bot,int right);
    void      Activate      ();
    void      Hide          ();
    void      Show          ();
    void      Clear         (int from = 1,int to = maxRows);
    void      GetLine       (char* str,int row);
    void      WriteStr      (const char* str,int len);
    void      ReadStr       (char* str,int len);

    Window& operator << (const char*);
    Window& operator << (char);
    Window& operator << (long);
    Window& operator << (double);
    Window& operator >> (char*);
    Window& operator >> (char&);
    Window& operator >> (long&);
    Window& operator >> (double&);
    friend  class Terminal;
};
#endif _WIND_
```

Window::Window (const char* title,int top,int left,int bot,int right)
Window::Window (const char* title,Rect& bounds)
The constructor first checks that an object of type `Terminal` has been created, and
makes a copy of the window `title`, if nonempty. The window is inserted in the
doubly-linked-list of windows and its `flags` is set to `hidden`. The area enclosed by
the window is initialized by calling `SetArea` (see below). The default pen position
for all windows is (1,1) and the default pen mode is a plain character pen.

───────────────────────── Window.cc ─────────────────────────

```
#include "Term.h"
#include "Wind.h"

Window::Window (const char* title,int top,int left,int bot,int right)
{
    if (Terminal::term == 0)
        Terminal::term->Error(termErr,"in Window");
    if (*title) {
        Window::title = new char[strlen(title) + 1];
        if (Window::title == 0)
            Terminal::term->Error(memErr,"for title");
        strcpy(Window::title,title);
    } else
        Window::title = 0;
    // insert in window list:
    prev = next = 0;
    if (Terminal::topWind == 0) {
        Terminal::botWind = this;
        Terminal::topWind = this;
    } else {
        Terminal::topWind->next = this;
        this->prev = Terminal::topWind;
        Terminal::topWind = this;
    }
    flags = hidden;
    SetArea(top,left,bot,right);
    PenPos(1,1);
    PenMode(defPen);
} /* Window */

inline
Window::Window (const char* title,Rect& bounds)
{
    Window(title,bounds.top,bounds.left,bounds.bot,bounds.right);
} /* Window */
```

void Window::SetArea (int top, int left, int bot, int right)
SetArea first checks the boundaries of a window, adjusting each if out of range. It
then allocates storage in area to represent every character position inside the
window as well as its border line characters. The graphical characters that make
up the border line and the window title are stored in area. Note that the window
is hidden at this stage: the screen appearance is unaffected by SetArea.

```
void
Window::SetArea (int top, int left, int bot, int right)
{
top = (top < 0 ? 0 : (top >= Terminal::rows ? Terminal::rows-1 : top));
left = (left < 0 ? 0 : (left >= Terminal::cols ? Terminal::cols-1 : left));
bot = (bot < top ? top : (bot >= Terminal::rows ? Terminal::rows-1 : bot));
right = (right < left ? left : (right >= Terminal::cols ? Terminal::cols-1
                                : right));
    bounds.Rect(top,left,bot,right);
    int height = bot - top + 1;
    int width = right - left + 1;
    register row, col;
    if ((area = new int[height * width]) == 0)
        Terminal::term->Error(memErr,"for area");
    register int* line = area;
    if (height >= 2 && width >= 2) {
        *line++ = topLeft | graphPen;           // draw upper border of window
        for (col = 1; col < width-1; ++col)
            *line++ = horizontal | graphPen;
        *line++ = topRight | graphPen;
        for (row = 1; row < height-1; ++row) {// draw middle of window
            *line++ = vertical | graphPen;
            for (col = 1; col < width-1; ++col) *line++ = ' ';
            *line++ = vertical | graphPen;
        }
        *line++ = botLeft | graphPen;           // draw lower border of window
        for (col = 1; col < width-1; ++col)
            *line++ = horizontal | graphPen;
        *line++ = botRight | graphPen;
    }
    if (title != 0) {                           // draw the title
        const char* name = title;
        line = area + 1;
        for (col = 1; col < width-1 && *name; ++col)
            *line++ = *name++ | revsPen;
    }
} /* SetArea */
```

Window::~Window ()
The destructor first hides a window if not already hidden. It then removes the
window from the doubly-linked-list of windows and deletes the storage occupied
by area and title.

void Window::PenPos (int row, int col)
Moves the pen (cursor) to the specified local coordinates. The coordinates are
automatically adjusted if they lie outside the window boundary. The cursor is
physically moved only when the window is visible.

void Window::PenMode (Mode pm)
Changes a window pen mode to the specified mode. Pm may specify more than
one mode at once. For example, to change the mode to graphics and reverse
video, the value (graphPen | revsPen) can be used.

```
Window::~Window()
{
    if (!Hidden())
        Hide();
    if (this == Terminal::botWind)
        Terminal::botWind = this->next;
    if (this == Terminal::topWind)
        Terminal::topWind = this->prev;
    if (this->next != 0)
        this->next->prev = this->prev;
    if (this->prev != 0)
        this->prev->next = this->next;
    delete area;
    delete title;
} /* ~Window */

void
Window::PenPos (int row, int col)
{
    pos.row = (row <= 0 ? 1 : (row >= bounds.bot - bounds.top ?
                               bounds.bot - bounds.top - 1 : row));
    pos.col = (col <= 0 ? 1 : (col >= bounds.right - bounds.left ?
                               bounds.right - bounds.left - 1 : col));
    if (!Hidden()) {
        PosCode(Terminal::termBuf,
                bounds.top+pos.row+1, bounds.left+pos.col+1);
        write(1, Terminal::termBuf, strlen(Terminal::termBuf));
    }
} /* PenPos */
```

void Window::Move (int row,int col)
Moves a window so that its top-left corner lies at the specified global coordinates. The coordinates are automatically adjusted if necessary. The window is moved by offsetting its boundary rectangle. This is sufficient if the window is currently invisible. Otherwise, the old and the new area covered by the window are refreshed.

```
void
Window::PenMode (Mode pm)
{
    if (!Hidden()) {
        if (pm & graphPen)
            Terminal::term->GraphPen();
        else
            Terminal::term->AlfaPen();
        if (pm & revsPen)
            Terminal::term->RevsPen();
        else
            Terminal::term->PlainPen();
    }
    mode = pm;
} /* PenMode */

void
Window::Move (int row,int col)
{
    int height = bounds.bot - bounds.top + 1;
    int width = bounds.right - bounds.left + 1;
    Rect oldBounds = bounds;
    row = (row < 0 ? 0 :
            (row+height > Terminal::rows ? Terminal::rows-height : row));
    col = (col < 0 ? 0 :
            (col+width > Terminal::cols ? Terminal::cols-width : col));
    if (row == bounds.top && col == bounds.left)
        return;
    row -= bounds.top;   col -= bounds.left;
    bounds.Offset(row,col);
    if (!Hidden()) {
        Terminal::term->Refresh(oldBounds);
        Terminal::term->Refresh(bounds,this);
        Terminal::curWind->Resume();
    }
} /* Move */
```

void Window::Resize (int top, int left, int bot, int right)
Changes the size of a window according to the new boundaries. If visible, the window is first hidden. Area is then deleted and recreated by calling SetArea. Finally, the pen is initialized and the visibility status of the window is restored.

void Window::Activate ()
Activates a window by making it visible and bringing it in front of all others. It has no effect if the window is already active. If the window is hidden, the refresh area (denoted by refBox) is set to the window boundaries and flags is modified to make the impression that the window is visible. Otherwise, the refresh area is calculated to be the smallest rectangle enclosing those parts of the window obstructed by other windows. In calculating this area only those visible windows that appear in front of the window are considered.

Next, the window is made the last window (denoted by topWind) in the doubly-linked-list of windows, and is set to be the current window (denoted by curWind). Refresh is called to redraw the calculated area and the window is resumed by calling Resume.

```
void
Window::Resize (int top, int left, int bot, int right)
{
    Bool visible = !Hidden();
    if (visible)
        Hide();
    delete area;
    SetArea(top, left, bot, right);
    PenPos(1,1);
    PenMode(defPen);
    if (visible)
        Show();
} /* Resize */

void
Window::Activate ()
{
    if (this == Terminal::curWind && !Hidden())
        return;
    Rect refBox;                 // refresh box
    if (Hidden()) {
        refBox = bounds;
        flags &= ~hidden;
    } else {
```

void Window::Hide ()

Hide has no effect if the window is already hidden. Otherwise, the corresponding
bit in flags is set and Refresh is called to redraw the area covered by the window.
This has the effect of displaying anything that has been obstructed by the
window. If this is the current window, the window appearing immediately
behind it is resumed instead. This is because a hidden window can never be the
current window.

```
    Rect rect = bounds, box;
    // refBox is initially empty:
    refBox.Rect(rect.bot,rect.right,rect.top,rect.left);
    // work out the overlapped area:
    for (Window* wind = this->next; wind != 0; wind = wind->next)
        if (!wind->Hidden() && !(box = rect * wind->bounds).Empty())
    refBox = box + refBox;
    }
    if (this != Terminal::topWind) {
        if (this->prev != 0)
            this->prev->next = this->next;
        else
            Terminal::botWind = this->next;
        this->next->prev = this->prev;
        this->next = 0;
        this->prev = Terminal::topWind;
        Terminal::topWind->next = this;
        Terminal::topWind = this;
    }
    Terminal::curWind = this;
    Terminal::term->Refresh(refBox,this);
    this->Resume();
} /* Activate */

void
Window::Hide ()
{
    if (Hidden())
        return;
    flags |= hidden;
    Terminal::term->Refresh(bounds);
    if (this == Terminal::curWind)
        this->prev->Resume();
} /* Hide */
```

void Window::Show ()

Show does the opposite of Hide and has no effect if the window is already visible. Otherwise, the corresponding bit in flags is reset and Refresh is called to redraw the window. The window is resumed if there is no current window or if the window is on top of the current window.

void Window::Resume ()

Resume makes a window the current window. However, if the window is hidden, the preceding window in the list is considered instead. This process is repeated until a visible window is found or until the start of the list is reached. In the latter case the cursor is moved to the last row of the screen, implying that no window is current.

```
void
Window::Show ()
{
    if (!Hidden())
        return;
    flags &= ~hidden;
    Terminal::term->Refresh(bounds,this);
    if (Terminal::curWind == 0)
        Resume();
    else // resume this if above curWind:
        for (Window* wind = Terminal::curWind; wind != 0; wind = wind->next)
            if (wind == this) Resume();
} /* Show */

void
Window::Resume ()
{
    Window* wind = this;
    while (wind != 0 && wind->Hidden())
        wind = wind->prev;
    if (wind == 0) {
        int lastRow = Terminal::rows;
        Terminal::term->PenPos(lastRow,1);
    } else {
        PenPos(pos.row,pos.col);
        PenMode(mode);
    }
    Terminal::curWind = wind;
} /* Resume */
```

void Window::Clear (int from = 1, int to = maxRows)
Clears the contents of a window line by line as specified by from and to. This has
no effect if the specified range is empty. From and to are adjusted automatically if
out of range. A blank line is built in buf and stamped onto the relevant lines.
The default arguments for this function have the effect of completely clearing
the contents of a window.

void Window::GetLine (char* str, int row)
Returns in str the contents of a line of the window as specified by row. Row is
expressed in local coordinates (e.g., row = 1 returns the first line inside the
window).

```
void
Window::Clear (int from, int to)
{
    int height = bounds.bot - bounds.top - 1;
    int width = bounds.right - bounds.left - 1;
    char *buf = Terminal::termBuf;
    if (from > to || from > height || to < 1)
        return;
    from = (from < 1 ? 1 : from);
    to = (to > height ? height : to);
    for (int col = 0; col < width; ++col)
        buf[col] = ' ';
    buf[col] = '\0';
    for (int row = from; row <= to; ++row) {
        PenPos (bounds.top+row, 1);
        WriteStr (buf, width);
    }
} /* Clear */

void
Window::GetLine (register char* str, int row)
{
    register width = bounds.right - bounds.left + 1;
    register int* line = area + row * width + 1;
    width -= 2;
    while (width-- > 0)
        *str++ = (char) *line++;
    *str = '\0';
} /* GetLine */
```

void Window::WriteStr (const char* string, int len)
Writes len characters from string to a window. The window does not have to be
the current window or even visible. The current pen position and pen mode for
the window are assumed. String is copied to the window character by character.
No actual writing takes place unless a \n character is encountered, or the end of a
window line is reached, in which case that portion of string is written and the
cursor is moved to the next line.

For a hidden window, only area is updated. For a visible window which is
not current (e.g., overlapped by another visible window) the actual writing is
performed by WriteBehind (see below). Reaching the end of a window causes the
writing to be continued from the beginning of the window. WriteStr does not
affect the order of windows.

```
void
Window::WriteStr (const char* string, int len)
{
    Bool visible = !Hidden();
    Bool current = this == Terminal::curWind;
    int  width = bounds.right - bounds.left + 1;
    int  room = width - pos.col - 1;
    int  col = pos.col;
    register const char* str = string;
    if (!current && visible) {
        PenPos (pos.row, pos.col);
        PenMode (mode);
    }
    for (register i = 0; i < len && *str ; ++i) {
        if (*str == '\n' || i >= room) {
            if (current) write (1, string, str - string);
            else if (visible) WriteBehind (string, pos.row, col, str - string);
            if (*str == '\n') ++str;
            else --i;
            string = str;
            if (pos.row >= bounds.bot-bounds.top-1) PenPos (1, col = 1);
            else PenPos (pos.row+1, col = 1);
            room += width - 2;
        } else
            *(area + pos.row * width + pos.col++) = *str++ | mode;
    }
    if (current) write (1, string, str - string);
    else if (visible) WriteBehind (string, pos.row, col, str - string);
    if (!current && visible)
        Terminal::curWind->Resume();
} /* WriteStr */
```

void Window::WriteBehind (const char* str, int row, int col, int len)
Writes len characters from str to a window, starting at the position denoted by row and col (expressed in local coordinates). WriteBehind is used for visible windows obstructed by other visible windows. It uses region to decide whether a character position corresponds to a visible part of the window. The number of write operations is minimized by breaking the string into a number of visible and invisible parts. Only the visible parts are written. Note that WriteBehind does not update area; this is the responsibility of the calling routine (see WriteStr).

void Window::ReadStr (char* string, int len)
Reads and returns in string at most len characters from a window. If not current, the window is first activated. Only printable characters are accepted as valid input. The input must be terminated by a \r or \n. The \b character is used for deleting erroneous input. Invalid characters are rejected by ringing the margin bell.

The output and input operators << and >> are implemented in terms of WriteStr and ReadStr and are self-explanatory. These can be easily extended to support other basic types such as short, int, and float.

```
void
Window::WriteBehind (register const char* str, int row, int col, int len)
{
    int width = bounds.right - bounds.left + 1;
    register Window** rgn = Terminal::region +
                (bounds.top + row) * Terminal::cols + bounds.left + col;
    register char* buf = Terminal::termBuf;
    int behind = 0;
    for (register i = 0; i < len; ++i) {
        if (*rgn++ == this) {
            if (behind > 0) {
                PosCode (buf, bounds.top+row+1, bounds.left+col+1+i);
                buf += strlen (buf);
                behind = 0;
            }
            *buf++ = *str++;
        } else
            ++behind;
    }
    write (1, Terminal::termBuf, buf - Terminal::termBuf);
} /* WriteBehind */
void
```

```
Window::ReadStr (char* string, int len)
{
    int width = bounds.right - bounds.left + 1;
    int room = width - pos.col - 1;
    int n = 0;
    Activate();
    int* line = area + pos.row * width + pos.col;
    room = (room < len ? room : len);
    for (;;) {
        int  key = Terminal::term->GetKey();
        char ch;
        if (n < room && isprint(key)) {
            *line++ = (string[n++] = key) | mode;
            write(0,&(ch = key),1);
            ++pos.col;
        } else if (key == '\r' || key == '\n') {
            break;
        } else if (key == '\b' && n > 0) {
            write(1,"\b",1);
            write(1,&(ch = ' '),1);
            *--line = (string[--n] = ' ') | mode;
            PenPos(pos.row,pos.col);
        } else
            Terminal::term->Bell();
    }
    string[n] = '\0';
} /* ReadStr */

Window&
Window::operator << (const char* str)
{
    WriteStr(str,strlen(str));
    return *this;
} /* operator << */

Window&
Window::operator << (char ch)
{
    windBuf[0] = ch;
    windBuf[1] = '\0';
    WriteStr(windBuf,1);
    return *this;
} /* operator << */
```

```
Window&
Window::operator << (long num)
{
    sprintf(windBuf,"%d",num);
    WriteStr(windBuf,strlen(windBuf));
    return *this;
} /* operator << */

Window&
Window::operator << (double num)
{
    sprintf(windBuf,"%f",num);
    WriteStr(windBuf,strlen(windBuf));
    return *this;
} /* operator << */

Window&
Window::operator >> (char* str)
{
    ReadStr(str,bounds.right - pos.col - 1);
    return *this;
} /* operator >> */

Window&
Window::operator >> (char& ch)
{
    ReadStr(windBuf,bounds.right - pos.col - 1);
    ch = windBuf[0];
    return *this;
} /* operator >> */

Window&
Window::operator >> (long& num)
{
    ReadStr(windBuf,bounds.right - pos.col - 1);
    num = atol(windBuf);
    return *this;
} /* operator >> */

Window&
Window::operator >> (double& num)
{
    ReadStr(windBuf,bounds.right - pos.col - 1);
    num = atof(windBuf);
    return *this;
} /* operator >> */
```

12.5 The Menu class

The Menu class is derived from the Window class and is useful for grouping a set of options from which the user may select. Menus can be static (remain permanently on the screen) or pop-up. The latter effect is obtained using the Hide and Show operations of the base class.

NOptions is the number of options in a menu, each option is displayed in one line. CurOptn denotes the current option (i.e., the one that the user is currently at). Action is a pointer to a function which is executed when an option is selected; this may be 0.

Menu inherits only 6 operations from Window; the remaining operations are irrelevant. The first 4 public members of Menu retrieve or alter certain attributes and are straightforward. The constructor and Select are the main operations.

```
                                        Menu.h
#ifndef _MENU_
#define _MENU_
#include "Common.h"

typedef int (*MenuAct) (Menu&, int);

class Menu : Window {
    int      nOptions;                   // number of options
    int      curOptn;                    // current option
    MenuAct  action;                     // menu action routine
    void     HiliteOption (int nOptn, Bool hilite);
public:
    Window::GetBounds;
    Window::Hidden;
    Window::Show;
    Window::Hide;
    Window::Activate;
    Window::Move;
    int      Options    ()                  { return nOptions; }
    int      CurOptn    ()                  { return curOptn; }
    void     SetAct     (MenuAct act)    { action = act; }
    void     GetAct     (MenuAct* act)    { *act = action; }
             Menu       (const char* title, int row, int col,
                                        MenuAct act, char* optn...);
    int      Select     (int start = 0, MenuAct escFun = 0);
};
#endif _MENU_
```

Menu::Menu (const char* title,int row,int col,MenuAct act,char* optn ...)
: (title,top,left,top,left)
Title is a title for the menu window. Row and col specify the window origin (its top-left corner) in global coordinates. Act is the action function to be executed after each option selection and may be 0. Optn is the first option of the menu; the list of options must be terminated by a 0.

_____Menu.cc_____

```
#include "Term.h"
#include "Wind.h"
#include "Menu.h"
#include <stdarg.h>

Menu::Menu (const char* title,int top,int left,MenuAct act,char* optn ...)
: (title,top,left,top,left)
{
    char*   optns[maxRows];
    register rows = 0, cols = 0, n;
    action = act;
    SetKind(menuWind);
    va_list arg;
    va_start(arg,optn);
    while (rows < Terminal::rows - 2) {
        optns[rows++] = optn;
        if ((n = strlen(optn)) > cols)
            cols = n;
        if ((optn = va_arg(arg,char*)) == 0)
            break;
    }
    va_end(arg);
    nOptions = rows;
    if (++cols + 2 > Terminal::cols)
        cols = Terminal::cols - 2;
    Resize(top,left,top+rows+1,left+cols+1);

    for (n = 1; n <= nOptions; ++n) {     // write the options
        PenPos(n,2);
        WriteStr(optns[n-1],cols - 1);
    }
    PenPos(1,1);
    HiliteOption(curOptn = 1,true);
} /* Menu */
```

The actual size of a menu window is calculated from the option strings. However, since arguments must be provided beforehand for the base class constructor, a window of size 0 is initially requested. The options are examined using va_arg and stored in the optns array until the final 0 is reached. The required window is of size $(n+1)*(m+2)$, where n is the number of options and m is the length of the longest option. The window is resized accordingly and the options are written to the window, each appearing on a separate line, starting from column 2. The first option is the default current option. This is highlighted by calling HiliteOptn. All menus are initially hidden.

void Menu::HiliteOptn (int nOptn, Bool hilite)
Highlights the option denoted by nOptn. The option is turned on (printed in reverse video) if hilite is true, and turned off (printed in plain video) otherwise. The print string is obtained by calling GetLine and after setting the pen mode, is written by calling WriteStr.

void Menu::Select (int start = 0, MenuAct escFun = 0)
Select allows the user to move up and down a menu and select an option. Start specifies the option to start at. If nonzero this option becomes the current option. EscFun is a function to be called when the user issues an escape command.

Select first activates the menu window and then uses a loop to respond to user commands. The up and down commands are used for moving, respectively, to the previous and the next option. Pressing the return key causes the current option to be selected and its number returned as the result. When action is non-zero, it is called as soon as a selection is made. A reference to the object and the option number are passed as arguments to action. In this way, action can respond differently to different options. The result returned by action is significant: a nonzero result means that the menu should be abandoned; otherwise, the menu remains active, allowing further options to be selected. EscFun is similar to action but is called when the user presses the escape key twice.

```
void
Menu::HiliteOption (int nOptn, Bool hilite)
{
    char optn [maxCols];
    Rect bounds;
    GetBounds (&bounds);
    GetLine (optn, nOptn);
    PenPos (nOptn, 1);    PenMode (hilite ? revsPen : defPen);
    WriteStr (optn, bounds.right - bounds.left - 1);
    PenPos (nOptn, 1);
} /* HiliteOption */
```

```
int
Menu::Select (int start,MenuAct escFun)
{
    if (start != 0 && start != curOptn) {
        HiliteOption(curOptn,false);
        HiliteOption(curOptn = start,true);
    }
    Activate();
    for (;;) {
        int optn = 0;
        int n = 0;

        switch (Terminal::term->GetKey()) {
          case upCmd:
                optn = (curOptn == 1 ? 0 : curOptn-1);
                break;
          case downCmd:
                optn = (curOptn == nOptions ? 0 : curOptn+1);
                break;
          case '\n':
          case '\r':
                n = curOptn;
                if (action == 0 || (n = (*action)(*this,n)) != 0)
                    return n;
                continue;
          case escCmd:
                n = curOptn;
                if (escFun != 0 && (n = (*escFun)(*this,n)) != 0)
                    return n;
                continue;
        } /* switch */

        if (optn == 0)
            Terminal::term->Bell();
        else {
            HiliteOption(curOptn,false);
            HiliteOption(curOptn = optn,true);
        }
    } /* for */
} /* Select */
```

12.6 The Form class

It is often desirable to group a set of closely related items together, allowing the user to manipulate them collectively. This is facilitated by electronic forms [Gehani 1983]. An electronic form is very similar to a paper form and consists of a number of fields which may be filled by the user in any order. A student enrollment form (containing fields such as name, address, enrollment number, courses taken, etc.) is a good example. Use of electronic forms has many advantages: they can ensure total consistency by automatically checking the values provided by the user, they can provide guidance as to how the form should be filled, and they can provide default values or even automatically fill those fields'that can be calculated from other fields.

The Form class is a simple realization of the electronic form concept and is derived from the Window class. A form object contains a set of fields. A Field consists of three items: a string of characters (data) representing the current value of the field, the position of the field in the form window (pos), and the length of the field (len). Fields is a dynamically allocated array of such fields, and nFields denotes the size of the array. TotLen is the total length of all fields put together. Action is a function executed before and after each field is filled by the user.

Form::Form (const char* title,int top,int left,FormAct act,char* line ...)
: (title,top,left,top,left)
The argument format for this constructor is similar to that of Menu. Line and subsequent arguments specify the contents of the form. The argument list must be terminated by a 0. Each line is an arbitrary string of characters. Consecutive underscore characters in each line are interpreted as a field, where the number of underscores determines the length of the field. Everything else is literal.

The actual size of a form window is calculated from the line strings. However, since arguments must be provided beforehand for the base class constructor, a window of size 0 is initially requested. The lines are examined using va_arg and then scanned character by character. For each encountered field, its details are stored in flds, and for each encountered literal, its details are stored in lits.

The window is resized to $(n+1)*(m+1)$ where n is the number of lines and m is the maximum line length. A string of length totLen is allocated, representing the form *image*. For each field, data is set to point to a portion of this string. Each field initially contains blanks and is terminated by a \t character. The last field is followed by a \0 character. The pen is initially positioned at the beginning of the first field. All forms are initially hidden.

Form::~Form ()
Simply deletes the string representing the data for the fields and fields itself.

_____Form.h_____

```
#ifndef _FORM_
#define _FORM_
#include "Common.h"
#include "Wind.h"
typedef int (*FormAct)(Form&,int);


struct Field {
    char*  data;                // data for the field (its value)
    Point  pos;                 // position of the field
    int    len;                 // field length
};


class Form : public Window {
    Field*  fields;             // form fields
    int     nFields;            // number of fields
    int     totLen;             // total length of all fields
    FormAct action;             // form action routine
    void HiliteField (int nFld,Bool hilite);
    void Drain        (int nFld);
public:
    int  Fields     ()                      { return nFields; }
    int  TotalLen   ()                      { return totLen; }
    int  FieldLen   (int nFld)              { return fields[nFld-1].len; }
    void SetAct     (FormAct act)           { action = act; }
    void GetAct     (FormAct* act)          { *act = action; }
         Form       (const char* title,int top,int left,
                                    FormAct act,char* name...);
        ~Form       ();
    void Read       (int nFld = 0,FormAct escFun = 0);
    void Update     (int nFld = 0);
    void Blank      (int nFld = 0);
    void SetValue   (int nFld,const char* val,Bool update = true);
    void SetValue   (int nFld,long val,Bool update = true);
    void SetValue   (int nFld,double val,Bool update = true);
    void SetAll     (const char* vals,Bool update = true);
    void GetValue   (int nFld,char* val,Bool truncate = false);
    void GetValue   (int nFld,long* val,Bool truncate = false);
    void GetValue   (int nFld,double* val,Bool truncate = false);
    void GetAll     (char* vals,Bool truncate = false);
};
#endif _FORM_
```

_____Form.cc_____

```cpp
#include "Term.h"
#include "Form.h"
#include <stdarg.h>


Form::Form (const char* title,int top,int left,FormAct act,char* line ...)
: (title,top,left,top,left)
{
    Field flds[maxFlds];
    Field lits[maxLits];
    int    totLen = 0;
    int    rows = 0, cols = 0;
    register n = 0, m = 0, i = 0;
    action = act;
    SetKind(formWind);

    va_list arg;
    va_start(arg,line);
    while (n < maxFlds && m < maxLits) {
        register char* str = line;
        while (*str) {
            if (*str == '_' && n < maxFlds) {
                flds[n].pos.row = rows + 1;
                flds[n].pos.col = str - line + 1;
                flds[n].len = 0;
                for (flds[n].len = 1; *++str == '_'; ++flds[n].len)
                    ;
                totLen += flds[n++].len + 1;
            } else if (m < maxLits) {
                lits[m].data = str;
                while (*++str != '\0' && *str != '_')
                    ;
                lits[m].pos.row = rows + 1;
                lits[m].pos.col = lits[m].data - line + 1;
                lits[m].len = str - lits[m].data;
                ++m;
            } else
                ++str;
        }
        ++rows;
        cols = (str - line > cols ? str - line : cols);
        if ((line = va_arg(arg,char*)) == 0)
```

```
            break;
        }
        va_end(arg);

        Resize(top,left,top+rows+1,left+cols+1);
        for (i = 0; i < m; ++i) {
            PenPos(lits[i].pos.row,lits[i].pos.col);
            WriteStr(lits[i].data,lits[i].len);
        }
        char* data;
        if ((data= new char[totLen + 1]) == 0)
            Terminal::term->Error(memErr,"in Form");
        for (i = 0; i < totLen; ++i)
            data[i] = ' ';
        data[totLen] = '\0';
        if ((fields = new Field[nFields = n]) == 0)
            Terminal::term->Error(memErr,"in Form");
        for (i = 0; i < n; ++i) {
            flds[i].data = data;
            data += flds[i].len + 1;
            *(data - 1) = '\t';
            fields[i] = flds[i];
        }
        PenPos(fields[0].pos.row,fields[0].pos.col);
} /* Form */

Form::~Form ()
{
    delete fields[0].data;
    delete fields;
} /* Form */

void
Form::HiliteField (int nFld,Bool hilite)
{
    if (nFld < 1 || nFld > nFields)
        return;
    Field& fld = fields[nFld-1];
    PenPos(fld.pos.row,fld.pos.col);
    PenMode(hilite ? revsPen : defPen);
    WriteStr(fld.data,fld.len);
    PenPos(fld.pos.row,fld.pos.col);
} /* HiliteField */
```

void Form::HiliteField (int nFld, Bool hilite)
Highlights the field denoted by nFld. The field is printed in reverse video if hilite is true, and in plain video otherwise.

void Form::Drain (int nFld)
Drains the data for the field denoted by nFld. The field becomes blank as a result.

void Form::Read (int nFld = 0, FormAct escFun = 0)
This function allows the user to interactively fill a form. When nFld is nonzero, only that field is allowed to be filled. Otherwise, the entire form may be filled. EscFun is a function and is executed when the user issues an escape command.

The form window is first activated. NFld is automatically adjusted if out of range, and the pen is moved to the requested field (or to the first field when nFld is 0). A loop is then used to respond to user commands. Pressing the up or the down arrow key moves the cursor, respectively, to the next or the previous field. Pressing the return key completes the data for the current field and causes the action function to be executed. If action returns a nonzero value, the form is exited. The tab key has the same effect as the down arrow key. The left and right arrow keys can be used for moving left and right within a field.

Erroneous input can be rubbed by pressing the backspace key. This causes the character to the left of the cursor to be erased. Pressing backspace at the beginning of a field erases the whole field. Pressing the escape key twice causes escFun to be executed. The result returned by this function is interpreted in the same way as action.

The default case in the switch statement deals with all other key presses. Nonprintable characters are ignored. Inputting the first character for a field causes the action function to be executed. Note that in this case the field number (denoted by nFld) is passed as a negative number. This tells action that the field is about to be filled (as opposed to: it has already been filled). An input data character is written at the current position of the cursor and stored in the data of the field. Read preserves the pen position and mode.

```
void
Form::Drain (int nFld)
{
    if (nFld < 1 || nFld > nFields)
        return;
    char* data = fields [nFld-1] .data;
    int    len = fields [nFld-1] .len;
    for (int i = 0; i < len; ++i)
        *data++ = ' ';
} /* Drain */
```

```
void
Form::Read (int nFld,FormAct escFun)
{
    Point pos;
    Mode mode;
    GetPos(&pos);
    GetMode(&mode);
    Activate();
    Bool readAll = nFld == 0;
    nFld = (nFld <= 0 ? 1 : (nFld > nFields ? nFields : nFld));
    Field* fld = &fields[nFld-1];
    PenPos(fld->pos.row,fld->pos.col);
    int key, next, idx = -1;
    char ch;

    for (;;) {
        switch (key = Terminal::term->GetKey()) {
            case upCmd:
                next = (readAll && nFld > 1 ? nFld-1 : 0);
                break;
            case '\n':
            case '\r':
                if (idx >= 0) HiliteField(nFld,false);
                idx = -1;
                if (action != 0 && (*action)(*this,nFld) != 0 || !readAll)
                    goto out;
            case '\t':
            case downCmd:
                next = (readAll && nFld < nFields ? nFld+1 : 0);
                break;
            case leftCmd:
                if (idx <= 0) Terminal::term->Bell();
                else PenPos(fld->pos.row,fld->pos.col + --idx);
                continue;
            case rightCmd:
                if (idx < 0) {
                    HiliteField(nFld,true);
                    idx = 0;
                }
                if (idx >= fld->len) Terminal::term->Bell();
                else PenPos(fld->pos.row,fld->pos.col + ++idx);
                continue;
            case '\b':
                if (idx < 0) {
                    for (int i = 0; i < fld->len; ++i)
```

```
                    fld->data[i] = ' ';
                    HiliteField(nFld,false);
                } else if (idx == 0) {
                    Terminal::term->Bell();
                } else {
                    for (int i = idx; i < fld->len; ++i)
                        fld->data[i-1] = fld->data[i];
                    fld->data[fld->len - 1] = ' ';
                    --idx;
                    write(1,"\b",1);
                    write(1,fld->data + idx,fld->len - idx);
                    PenPos(fld->pos.row,fld->pos.col + idx);
                }
                continue;
            case escCmd:
                if (idx >= 0) HiliteField(nFld,false);
                if (escFun == 0 || (*escFun)(*this,nFld) != 0) goto out;
                continue;
            default:
                if (!isprint(key) || idx >= fld->len) {
                    Terminal::term->Bell();
                    continue;
                }
                if (++idx == 0) {
                    if (action != 0 && (*action)(*this,-nFld) != 0)
                        continue;
                    HiliteField(nFld,true); ++idx;
                }
                write(1,&(ch = key),1);
                *(fld->data + idx - 1) = ch;
                continue;
        } /* switch */
        if (next == 0) Terminal::term->Bell();
        else {
            if (idx >= 0) HiliteField(nFld,false);
            fld = &fields[(nFld = next) -1];
            PenPos(fld->pos.row,fld->pos.col);
            idx = -1;
        }
    } /* for */
out:
    PenPos(pos.row,pos.col);
    PenMode(mode);
} /* Read */
```

void Form::Update (int nFld = 0)
Updates the field denoted by nFld. When nFld is 0 all fields are updated. Updating
a field simply causes the data for the field to be written (in plain video). Update is
usually called after a direct change to the data of one or more fields. Update
preserves the pen position and mode.

void Form::Blank (int nFld = 0)
Clears the field denoted by nFld. When nFld is 0 all fields are cleared. Blank
preserves the pen position and mode.

```
void
Form::Update (register nFld)
{
    Point pos;
    Mode mode;
    GetPos (&pos);
    GetMode (&mode);
    if (nFld <= 0)
        for (nFld = 1; nFld <= nFields; ++nFld) HiliteField(nFld,false);
    else if (nFld <= nFields)
        HiliteField(nFld,false);
    PenPos (pos.row,pos.col);
    PenMode (mode);
} /* Update */

void
Form::Blank (register nFld)
{
    Point pos;
    Mode mode;
    GetPos (&pos);
    GetMode (&mode);
    if (nFld <= 0) {
        for (nFld = 1; nFld <= nFields; ++nFld) {
            Drain (nFld);
            HiliteField(nFld,false);
        }
    } else if (nFld <= nFields) {
        Drain (nFld);
        HiliteField(nFld,false);
    }
    PenPos (pos.row,pos.col);
    PenMode (mode);
} /* Blank */
```

void Form::SetValue (int nFld, const char* val, Bool update = true)
void Form::SetValue (int nFld, long val, Bool update = true)
void Form::SetValue (int nFld, double val, Bool update = true)
Sets the value for the field denoted by nFld according to val. The field is also updated when update is true. Long and double values are converted to string format first. Values shorter than the field are right-padded with blanks. A string val must be terminated by a \t or a \0.

void Form::SetAll (const char* vals, Bool update = true)
Sets the values for all fields according to vals. The fields are also updated when update is true. Vals should contain values for all fields, each terminated by a \t. The values 'may be shorter than the fields, in which case they are right-padded with blanks. SetAll is useful for changing all the contents of a form at once.

```
void
Form::SetValue (int nFld,register const char* val,Bool update)
{
    if (nFld >= 1 && nFld <= nFields) {
        register char* data = fields[nFld-1].data;
        while (*val && *val != '\t' && *data != '\t')
            *data++ = *val++;
        while (*data != '\t')
            *data++ = ' ';
        if (update)
            HiliteField(nFld,false);
    }
} /* SetValue */

void
Form::SetValue (int nFld,long val,Bool update)
{
    char data[maxCols];
    sprintf(data,"%d",val);
    SetValue(nFld,data,update);
} /* SetValue */

void
Form::SetValue (int nFld,double val,Bool update)
{
    char data[maxCols];
    sprintf(data,"%f",val);
    SetValue(nFld,data,update);
} /* SetValue */
```

```
void
Form::SetAll (register const char* vals,Bool update)
{
    for (register nFld = 0; nFld < nFields; ++nFld) {
        register char* data = fields[nFld].data;
        while (*vals && *vals != '\t' && *data != '\t') *data++ = *vals++;
        while (*vals && *vals != '\t') ++vals;
        if (*vals == '\t') ++vals;
        while (*data != '\t') *data = ' ';
    }
    if (update) Update();
} /* SetAll */

void
Form::GetValue (int nFld,register char* val,Bool truncate)
{
    if (nFld < 1 || nFld > nFields) {
        *val = '\0';
        return;
    }
    register const char* data = fields[nFld-1].data;
    while (*data != '\t') *val++ = *data++;
    if (truncate) {
        while (*--val == ' ') ;
        ++val;
    }
    *val = '\0';
} /* GetValue */

void
Form::GetValue (int nFld,long* val,Bool truncate)
{
    char data[maxCols];
    GetValue(nFld,data,truncate);
    *val = atol(data);
} /* GetValue */

void
Form::GetValue (int nFld,double* val,Bool truncate)
{
    char data[maxCols];
    GetValue(nFld,data,truncate);
    *val = atof(data);
} /* GetValue */
```

```
void Form::GetValue (int nFld, char* val, Bool truncate = false)
void Form::GetValue (int nFld, long* val, Bool truncate = false)
void Form::GetValue (int nFld, double* val, Bool truncate = false)
```
Copies the value of the field denoted by nFld into val. The padding banks to the
right of the field are stripped when truncate is true. The field is converted to the
type to which val points.

```
void Form::GetAll (char* vals, Bool truncate = false)
```
Copies the values of all fields into vals. The padding banks to the right of the
fields are stripped when truncate is true. Each value in vals is terminated by a \t.
The last field is followed by a \0.

This concludes the description of the UIM facilities. It is worth pointing out
that the C++ version of this program was derived from an earlier C version
[Hekmatpour 1989]. Comparison of these two reveals that the C++ version is
much easier to understand and yet more complete. The improved quality is
mainly due to the neat breakdown and protection facilitated by classes, and the
use of constructors and destructors which guarantee proper initialization and
reclamation of objects.

Recoding the program in C++, however, was not straightforward and
required most of the program to be completely redesigned. This confirms the
contention that object-oriented design is fundamentally different from
functional decomposition [Booch 1986].

```
void
Form::GetAll (register char* vals, Bool truncate)
{
    for (register nFld = 0; nFld < nFields; ++nFld) {
        register const char* data = fields[nFld].data;
        while (*data != '\t') *vals++ = *data++;
        if (truncate) {
            while (*--vals == ' ') ;
            ++vals;
        }
        *vals++ = '\t';
    }
    *vals = '\0';
} /* GetAll */
```

12.7 Application program example

This section illustrates how the UIM is used. It describes a simple application program for maintaining a list of publications. The details of each publication are kept in a file. The program provides a window-based user interface for creating new publication entries, removing old entries, and searching through the list.

Each publication is stored as the image of an electronic form which describes that publication. The images are organized as a linked-list, where each entry in the list is of type `Article`. In a realistic implementation one would use a more efficient data structure (e.g., a B-tree).

```
#include <builtin.h>
#include <stdio.h>
#include "Term.h"
#include "Wind.h"
#include "Menu.h"
#include "Form.h"
struct Article {
    Article* next;                  // pointer to the next article in the list
    char image[1];                  // article image (allocated dynamically)
};
class ArticleDB {
    const maxSelect = 20;           // max no. of selected articles
    char*    fileName;              // DB file name
    Article* articles;             // linked-list of articles
    Article* select[maxSelect];    // selected articles
    int      nSelect;              // no. of selected articles
    int      curSel;               // currently selected article
    static   char artBuf[bufSize];  // article buffer
    Bool     update;               // update flag
    Bool     Match       (const char* pattern, const char* image);
public:
    int      Selected    ()            { return nSelect; }
    int      CurSelect   ()            { return curSel; }
    void     ZeroSelect  ()            { nSelect = curSel = 0; }
             ArticleDB   (const char* fName);
             ~ArticleDB  ();
    Bool     Insert      (const char* image);
    Bool     Delete      ();
    int      Search      (const char* pattern);
    char*    PrevImage   ();
    char*    CurImage    ();
    char*    NextImage   ();
    void     SetImage    (const char* image);
};
```

The article database is defined as a class called `ArticleDB`. `FileName` is the name of the file in which the article images are stored. `Articles` is a pointer to the beginning of the linked-list of articles. `Select` is an array of pointers to articles that are currently selected. `NSelect` is the number of selected articles, and `curSel` is the current article in the selection. `ArtBuf` is a private buffer for I/O purposes. `Update` is a flag which is set to true when the article file requires updating.

ArticleDB::ArticleDB (const char* fName)
The constructor allocates storage for and copies the file name, and reads the article images in the file. A linked-list of the images is constructed in `articles`.

ArticleDB::~ArticleDB ()
When `update` is true, the destructor writes the article images to the file. It also deletes the storage allocated for the file name and the entries in the linked-list.

Bool ArticleDB::Insert (const char* image)
Inserts the article denoted by `image` in the front of the linked-list of articles. `Insert` returns false when successful, and true otherwise.

Bool ArticleDB::Delete ()
Deletes the currently selected article (denoted by `curSel`) from the linked-list of articles. The article is also deleted from the array of selected articles. `Delete` returns false when successful, and true otherwise.

int ArticleDB::Search (const char* pattern)
Searches the list of articles, selecting all articles that match `pattern`. `Search` returns the number of selected articles.

Bool ArticleDB::Match (const char* pattern, const char* image)
Returns true if `image` matches `pattern`, and false otherwise. `Pattern` should have the same structure as image: it should consist of a sequence of fields, each terminated by a \t. A field in `pattern` matches the corresponding field in `image` if the former is a substring of the latter.

char* ArticleDB::PrevImage ()
char* ArticleDB::CurImage ()
char* ArticleDB::NextImage ()
Return, respectively, the previous, current, and the next article image from the set of selected articles.

```
ArticleDB::ArticleDB (const char* fName)
{
    fileName = new char[strlen(fName) + 1];
    strcpy(fileName,fName);
    articles = 0;
    nSelect = curSel = 0;
    FILE* file = fopen(fName,"r");
    if (file != 0) {
        while (fgets(artBuf,bufSize,file) != 0) {
            int len = strlen(artBuf);
            artBuf[--len] = '\0';                    // replace \n by \0
            Article* art = (Article*) new char[sizeof(Article) + len];
            art->next = articles;
            strcpy(art->image,artBuf);
            articles = art;
        }
        fclose(file);
    }
} /* ArticleDB */

ArticleDB::~ArticleDB ()
{
    if (update) {
        FILE* file = fopen(fileName,"w");
        if (file != 0) {
            for (Article* art = articles; art != 0; art = art->next)
                if (fputs(art->image,file) <= 0 || fputs("\n",file) <= 0)
                    break;
            fclose(file);
        }
    }
    delete fileName;
    while (articles != 0) {
        Article* temp = articles;
        articles = articles->next;
        delete temp;
    }
} /* ArticleDB */
```

```
Bool
ArticleDB::Insert (const char* image)
{
    Article* art;
    for (art = articles; art != 0; art = art->next)
        if (strcmp(image,art->image) == 0)
            return true;
    art = (Article*) new char[sizeof(Article) + strlen(image)];
    strcpy(art->image,image);
    art->next = articles;
    articles = art;
    return false;
} /* Insert */

Bool
ArticleDB::Delete ()
{
    if (curSel == 0)
        return true;
    Article* article = select[curSel-1];
    if (article == articles) {
        articles = articles->next;
        delete article;
    } else {
        for (Article* art = articles; art->next != 0; art = art->next)
            if (article == art->next) {
                art->next = art->next->next;
                delete article;
                goto out;
            }
        return true;
    }
  out:
    for (int n = 0; n < nSelect; ++n)
        if (select[n] == article) {
            --nSelect;
            for (; n < nSelect; ++n)
                select[n] = select[n+1];
            break;
        }
    return false;
} /* Delete */
```

```
int
ArticleDB::Search (const char* pattern)
{
    nSelect = 0;
    for (Article* art=articles; art!=0 && nSelect<maxSelect; art=art->next)
        if (Match(pattern,art->image))
            select[nSelect++] = art;
    curSel = (nSelect > 0 ? 1 : 0);
    return nSelect;
} /* Search */

Bool
ArticleDB::Match (const char* pattern, const char* image)
{
    while (*pattern) {
        Bool match = false;
        int len = 0;
        for (const char* str = pattern; *str != '\t'; ++str) ++len;
        while (*image != '\t')
            if (strncmp(pattern,image++,len) == 0) {
                match = true;
                break;
            }
        if (!match) return false;
        while (*image++ != '\t') ;
        while (*pattern++ != '\t') ;
    }
    return true;
} /* Match */

char*
ArticleDB::PrevImage ()
{ return (curSel <= 1 || nSelect == 0 ? 0 : select[--curSel-1]->image); }

char*
ArticleDB::CurImage ()
{ return (nSelect == 0 ? 0 : select[curSel-1]->image); }

char*
ArticleDB::NextImage ()
{ return (curSel < nSelect ? select[curSel++]->image : 0); }
```

char* ArticleDB::SetImage (const char* image)
Sets the image of the currently selected article (if any) to image.

void Display (Terminal& term, Form& article,
               const char* image, int idx, int total)
Displays image in the form denoted by article. Idx is the index of this image in
the set of total selected articles. Image is copied to article by calling SetAll and a
message is displayed to that effect.

main ()
An object of type Terminal is first defined; this is necessary. The article database db
is defined to correspond to the file articleDB. The commands menu contains a list
of commands directly corresponding to the ones appearing in the MenuCmds
enumeration. This is followed by the article form. The commands offered by
the menu are handled by a loop and a switch statement. Each time round the
loop, Select is called, allowing the user to select a command.

The newTemplateCmd clears the current selection, clears the contents of the
article form, clears the message line, and reads a new article image. In contrast,
the editTemplateCmd only reads a new article image.

The searchCmd searches the article list only when the current selection is
empty. The current contents of the form is used as a pattern for the search. This
is copied into buffer and forwarded to Search. The result of the search is
displayed by calling Display. The previousCmd and the nextCmd display,
respectively, the image preceding and the image succeeding the currently selected
article.

```
void
ArticleDB::SetImage (const char* image)
{
    if (curSel > 0)
        strcpy(select[curSel-1]->image, image);
}

void
Display (Terminal& term, Form& article, const char* image, int idx, int total)
{
    if (image != 0) {
        article.SetAll(image);
        term.Message(form("%d of %d", idx, total));
    } else
        term.Bell();
} /* Display */
```

The `saveArticleCmd` gets the current image in `article` and inserts it in the linked-list of article images. If this article is also selected then it is simply substituted (this is useful for modifying old articles). The `deleteArticleCmd` deletes the current article image from the linked-list of article images. If successful, the selected image preceding or succeeding the article (as appropriate) is displayed instead. The form is made blank if no such image exists.

Finally, the `quitCmd` sets `quit` to true, thereby terminating the application program.

```
enum MenuCmds { none, newTemplateCmd, editTemplateCmd,
                searchCmd, previousCmd, nextCmd5,
                saveArticleCmd, deleteArticleCmd7, quitCmd
};

main ()
{
    Terminal term;
    ArticleDB db("articleFile");
    char buffer[bufSize];
    Menu commands("",0,0,0,
                  "New Template","Edit Template","Search","Previous Image",
                  "Next Image","Save Article","Delete Article","Quit",0);
    Form article("Article",5,20,0,
                 "AUTHOR:      _____  ENTERED:  _____",
                 "TITLE:       _____",
                 "PERIODICAL:  _____",
                 "VOLUME:      ___   NUMBER: ___   YEAR:    _____",
                 "PUBLISHER:   _____  PLACE:    _____",
                 0);
    article.Show();
    Bool quit = false;

    while (!quit) {
        switch (commands.Select()) {
            case newTemplateCmd:
                db.ZeroSelect();
                article.Blank();
                term.Message("");
                article.Read();
                break;
            case editTemplateCmd:
                article.Read();
                break;
```

```
          case searchCmd:
                  if (db.Selected() == 0) {
                      article.GetAll(buffer,true);
                      db.Search(buffer);
                      Display(term,article,db.CurImage(),
                              db.CurSelect(),db.Selected());
                  }
                  break;
          case previousCmd:
                  Display(term,article,db.PrevImage(),
                          db.CurSelect(),db.Selected());
                  break;
          case nextCmd:
                  Display(term,article,db.NextImage(),
                          db.CurSelect(),db.Selected());
                  break;
          case saveArticleCmd:
                  article.GetAll(buffer,false);
                  if (db.CurSelect() != 0) {
                      db.SetImage(buffer);
                      term.Message("Substituted");
                  } else if (db.Insert(buffer)) {
                      term.Message("Duplicate!");
                      term.Bell();
                  } else
                      term.Message("Saved");
                  break;
          case deleteArticleCmd:
                  if (db.Delete()) {
                      term.Message("No selection!");
                      term.Bell();
                  } else {
                      char* image;
                      if ((image = db.CurImage()) != 0 ||
                          (image = db.PrevImage()) != 0)
                          Display(term,article,image,
                                  db.CurSelect(),db.Selected());
                      else
                          article.Blank();
                  }
                  break;
         case quitCmd: quit = true;
     }
   } /* while */
} /* main */
```

Figure 12.2 shows a screen view of the user interface during a search operation.

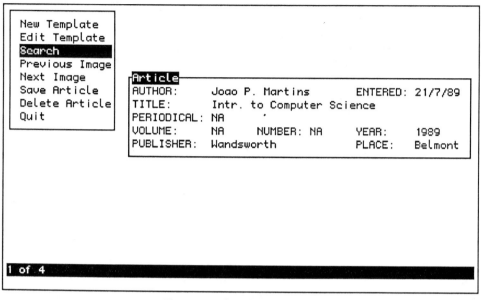

Figure 12.2 Searching for a title.

12.8 Summary

A **User Interface Manager** (UIM) provides abstractions for user interface design and can significantly reduce the time and cost of development. Use of a UIM requires only a knowledge of what each facility does, but not how it works.

Modern **user interfaces** are window-based and mouse-driven. Windows facilitate the provision of a number of independent workspaces on one screen.

A **window** is conveniently defined as a class. Overloading the I/O operators enable us to treat a window as a stream.

A **menu** is useful for grouping a set of options from which the user may choose. Since a menu is usually displayed in a window, it is defined as a derived class.

An electronic **form** is similar to a paper form and is used for grouping a set of closely related items, allowing the user to manipulate them collectively. Forms are also window-based and hence defined as a derived class.

CHAPTER 13

Case Study: Word Processing

This final case study describes the development of a number of classes for use in a word processing application. The aim of the study is to illustrate the use of multiple inheritance in C++. After describing some simple classes for representing lines, raw text, and rulers, we derive a number of classes to represent more abstract objects such as formatted scripts, tables, and paragraphs. The derivations also illustrate the use of virtual base classes.

13.1 Introduction

A **word processor** is an application program that supports the composition of formatted text by naive end-users. It is different from a **text formatter** in the sense that formatting is done on the fly so that the text shown on the screen is a good approximation of the final outcome.

In a text formatter, formatting instructions are inserted in the raw text as commands. The text formatter scans the text, interprets the commands and formats the text accordingly, producing an output which is then printed on a printer. In a word processor, on the other hand, formatting instructions are issued by the user at run-time (by, for example, choosing commands from a menu or clicking the mouse in a palette).

In both cases, text is composed out of successively larger units: a line is made up of words, a paragraph is made up of lines, a section is made up of paragraphs, etc. A word processor developed using object-oriented programming would implement these units as classes. Our aim here is to develop a number of such classes and to document their relationships using single and multiple inheritance.

As in the previous chapter, to facilitate separate compilation, we break each class into its declaration and implementation parts and store them in separate files. The code presented in this chapter consists of the following files:

FILE	CONTENTS
Consts.h	constants and enumerations shared by all files
Line.h	declaration of the Line class
Text.h	declaration of the Text class
Ruler.h	declaration of the Ruler class
Buffer.h	declaration of the Buffer class
Script.h	declaration of the Script class
Grid.h	declaration of the Grid class
Table.h	declaration of the Table class
Paragraph.h	declaration of the Paragraph class
Line.cc	implementation of the Line class
Text.cc	implementation of the Text class
Ruler.cc	implementation of the Ruler class
Buffer.cc	implementation of the Buffer class
Script.cc	implementation of the Script class
Grid.cc	implementation of the Grid class
Table.cc	implementation of the Table class
Paragraph.cc	implementation of the Paragraph class

The contents of Consts.h is as shown below.

―――――――――――――――――――――Consts.h―――――――――――――――――――――
```
#ifndef _CONSTS_
#define _CONSTS_

enum Bool    {false,true};
enum Indent   {leftInd,centerInd,rightInd};   // indentation modes
enum ParKind {script,table};                  // paragraph kind

#define maxWordSize    32     // maximum word size
#define maxRMargin     80     // maximum right margin
#define bufLines       64     // number of buffer lines
#define maxRows        32     // maximum number of grid rows
#define maxCols        10     // maximum number of grid columns
#define maxItem        32     // maximum length of grid item

#endif _CONSTS_
```

13.2 Line, Text, and Ruler

A line of words is represented by an object of type `Line`. Although a line may be empty, at least `minSize` bytes are allocated (in `data`) for representing the contents of the line. `Size` denotes the size of the block pointed to by `data`. `Used` denotes the number of bytes used from this block. `WordPos` is an index to the beginning of the next word in the line. This is used by the iterator function `GetWord` for returning the next word in the line.

Line::Line (const char* str = "")
The constructor allocates storage for `str` and copies `str` to `data`. When `str` is longer than `minSize` bytes, an extra `minSize` bytes is allocated to avoid further allocation should the line expand later on. All lines are null-terminated.

Line.h

```
#ifndef _LINE_
#define _LINE_
#include "Consts.h"
#include <ctype.h>
#include <stream.h>


class Line {
      const   minSize = 20;       // minimum storage allocated for data
      char*   data;               // line data, indices start at 0
      short   size;               // size of data
      short   used;               // number of chars used in data
      short   wordPos;            // current word position (for GetWord)
public:
              Line      (const char* str = "");
              ~Line     ()              { delete data; }
      void    Insert    (short from, short to, const char* str = "");
      Bool    Empty     ();
      Bool    GetWord   (char* word);
      friend  istream& operator >> (istream& in, Line& line);
      friend  ostream& operator << (ostream& out, Line& line);
};
#endif _LINE_
```

Line.cc

```
#include "Line.h"
Line::Line (const char* str)
{
      used = strlen(str);
      size = used + 1 > minSize ? used + minSize : minSize;
      data = new char[size];      strcpy(data, str);
} /* Line */
```

```
// replace from...to (excluding to) in a line by str:

void
Line::Insert (short from, short to, const char* str)
{
    from = from < 0 ? 0 : from;
    to = to > used ? used : to;
    if (from > to)
        return;
    int lost = to - from;

    int len = strlen(str);
    char* old = 0;
    if (len + used - lost >= size-1) {                      // enlarge
        old = data;
        data = new char[size += minSize];
    } else if (size -len - used + lost >= minSize) {   // reduce
        old = data;
        data = new char[size -= minSize];
    }
    if (old != 0) {                                         // rebuild line
        if (from > 0)                                       // left part
            strncpy (data, old, from);
        if (len > 0)                                        // middle part
            strncpy (data+from, str, len);
        if (to < used)                                      // right part
            strncpy (data+from+len, old+to, used-to);
        delete old;
    } else {
        int i;
        if (lost < len)
            for (i = used; i >= to; --i)                    // shift right
                data[i+len-lost] = data[i];
        else
            for (i = to; i < used; ++i)                     // shift left
                data[i+len-lost] = data[i];
        strncpy (data+from, str, len);
    }
    used += len - lost;
    data[used] = '\0';
} /* Insert */
```

void Line::Insert (short from, short to, const char* str = "")
This function inserts the string denoted by str so that it replaces the line characters starting (inclusive) at from and ending (exclusive) at to. Insert can be used for inserting into a line (when from = to), deleting from a line (when from < to and str is empty), or replacing a portion of a line with a new string (when from < to and str is nonempty).

Insert enlarges the block denoted by data when it is not large enough to accommodate an insertion, and reduces the block when the number of unused bytes in the block exceeds minSize.

Bool Line::Empty ()
Empty returns true if and only if a line is empty. A line is considered to be empty if it contains no characters at all or only blank characters.

Bool Line::GetWord (char* word)
GetWord copies the next word of the line (its position denoted by wordPos) to word. It returns true if the word is nonempty. Otherwise, it resets wordPos to the beginning of the line and returns false.

The operators >> and << are overloaded for the input and output of a line with respect to a stream. The implementation of these is self-explanatory.

```
Bool
Line::Empty ()
{
    for (char* str = data; *str != '\0'; ++str)
        if (!isspace(*str)) return false;
    return true;
} /* Empty */


Bool
Line::GetWord (char* word)
{
    while (wordPos < used && isspace(data[wordPos]))    // skip blanks
        ++wordPos;
    for (int i = 0; i < maxWordSize &&                  // copy the word
                    wordPos < used &&
                    !isspace(data[wordPos]); ++i)
        word[i] = data[wordPos++];
    word[i] = '\0';
    if (i == 0) wordPos = 0;                            // reset
    return i > 0;
} /* GetWord */
```

```
istream&
operator >> (istream& in,Line& line)
{
    char buf[256];
    in >> buf;
    line.used = strlen(buf);
    line.wordPos = 0;
    if (line.used >= line.size) {
        delete line.data;
        line.data = new char[line.size = line.used + Line::minSize];
    }
    strcpy(line.data,buf);
    return in;
} /* operator >> */

ostream&
operator << (ostream& out,Line& line)
{
    out << line.data;
    return out;
} /* operator << */
```
_____Text.h_____
```
#ifndef _TEXT_
#define _TEXT_
#include "Line.h"
#include <stream.h>

class Text {
    const    minSize = 4;          // minimum number of lines in a Text
    typedef Line* LinPtr;
    LinPtr* lines;                 // lines vector, indices start at 0
    short    size;                 // number of lines in 'lines'
    short    used;                 // number of used lines
    short    wordLine;             // the line holding the current word
public:
            Text     ();
            ~Text    ();
    void    NewLine  (short pos,Line* line);
    void    RmvLine  (short pos);
    void    Insert   (short pos,short from,short to,const char* str = "");
    Bool    GetWord  (char* word);
    friend  istream& operator >> (istream& in,Text& text);
    friend  ostream& operator << (ostream& out,Text& text);
};
#endif _TEXT_
```

A `Text` object represents a piece of raw text (i.e., unformatted) and consists of zero or more lines. The lines are denoted by `lines` which is a pointer to a vector of `Line` pointers. `Size` denotes the number of line pointers in `lines`. `Used` denotes the number of pointers in `lines` that are actually used. `WordLine` is an index to the `lines` vector and denotes the line containing the current word. This is used by the iterator function `GetWord` for returning the next word in the text.

Text.cc

```
#include "Text.h"

Text::Text ()
{
    lines = new LinPtr[size = minSize];
    for (int i = 0; i < size; ++i)
        lines[i] = 0;
    used = wordLine = 0;
} /* Text */

Text::~Text ()
{
    for (int i = 0; i < used; ++i)
        delete lines[i];
    delete lines;
} /* ~Text */

void
Text::NewLine (short pos,Line* line)
{
    pos = pos < 0 ? 0 : (pos > used ? used : pos);
    Line** old = 0;
    if (used == size) {
        old = lines;
        lines = new LinPtr[size += minSize];
        for (int i = 0; i < pos; ++i)         // copy
            lines[i] = old[i];
        for (i = pos+1; i <= used; ++i)       // shift down
            lines[i] = old[i-1];
        for (i = used+1; i < size; ++i)       // null lines
            lines[i] = 0;
    } else
        for (int i = used; i > pos; --i)      // shift down
            lines[i] = lines[i-1];
    lines[pos] = line;
    ++used;
} /* NewLine */
```

Text::Text ()
The constructor allocates minSize Line pointers in lines and initializes all
pointers to 0.

Text::~Text ()
The destructor deletes the Line objects denoted by the lines vector and then
deletes lines itself.

void Text::NewLine (short pos, Line* line)
NewLine inserts line in lines at the position denoted by pos. When lines is full,
its size is increased by minSize.

void Text::RmvLine (short pos)
RmvLine removes the line denoted by pos in lines. When the number of unused
pointers in lines exceeds minSize, the size of the vector is reduced by minSize.

```
void
Text::RmvLine (short pos)
{
    if (used == 0)
        return;
    pos = pos < 0 ? 0 : (pos >= used ? used-1 : pos);
    Line** old = 0;
    delete lines[pos];
    --used;
    if (size - used > minSize) {
        old = lines;
        lines = new LinPtr[size -= minSize];
        for (int i = 0; i < pos; ++i)          // copy
            lines[i] = old[i];
        for (i = pos; i <= used; ++i)          // shift up
            lines[i] = old[i+1];
        for (i = used+1; i < size; ++i)        // null lines
            lines[i] = 0;
        delete old;
    } else {
        for (int i = pos; i < used; ++i)       // shift up
            lines[i] = lines[i+1];
        lines[used] = 0;
    }
} /* RmvLine */
```

```
void
Text::Insert (short pos,short from,short to,const char* str)
{
    if (pos >= 0 && pos < used)
          lines[pos]->Insert(from,to,str);
} /* Insert */

Bool
Text::GetWord (char* word)
{
    if (wordLine < used) {
          if (lines[wordLine]->GetWord(word))
                return true;
          ++wordLine;
          return GetWord(word);
    }
    wordLine = 0;          // reset
    return false;
} /* GetWord */

istream&
operator >> (istream& in,Text& text)
{
    Line* line;
    for (;;) {
          line = new Line;
          in >> *line;
          if (line->Empty()) {
                delete line;
                return in;
          }
          text.NewLine(text.used,line);
    }
} /* operator >> */

ostream&
operator << (ostream& out,Text& text)
{
    for (int i = 0; i < text.used; ++i)
      out << *(text.lines[i]) << "\n";
    return out;
} /* operator << */
```

void Text::Insert (short pos, short from, short to, const char* str = "")
This function inserts the string denoted by `str` in the line denoted by `pos`. See
`Line::Insert` above.

Bool Text::GetWord (char* word)
`GetWord` copies the next word of the line denoted by `wordLine` to `word`. It returns
true if the word is nonempty. Otherwise, it resets `wordLine` to the first line and
returns false. See `Line::GetWord` above.

The operators >> and << are overloaded for the input and output of a text
with respect to a stream. These are implemented in terms of their `Line`
counterparts.

A `Ruler` object represents a means of specifying margins, tabs positions, and
indentation modes for a piece of text. The left and right margins are, respectively,
denoted by `lMargin` and `rMargin`. A ruler may specify up to 10 tab positions; these
are stored in `tabs`. The indentation mode is denoted by `indent` and may be one of
`leftInd`, `centerInd`, or `rightInd`.

Ruler::Ruler ()
The constructor initializes the margins, the tab positions, and the indentation
mode. The default indentation mode is `leftInd`.

Ruler.h

```
#ifndef _RULER_
#define _RULER_
#include "Consts.h"
#include <stdarg.h>

class Ruler {
protected:
    short    lMargin;
    short    rMargin;
    short    tabs[10];
    Indent   indent;    // indentation
public:
         Ruler          ();
    void Margins        (short lMarg = 0, short rMarg = maxRMargin);
    void Tabs           (short tab1 ...);
    void Indentation (Indent ind)        { indent = ind; }
};
#endif _RULER_
```

void Ruler::Margins (short lMarg = 0, short rMarg = maxRMargin)
This function sets the margins for a ruler.

void Ruler::Tabs (short tab1 ...)
Tabs sets the ruler tab positions. When less than 10 tabs are specified, the last
argument to Tabs must be a zero, marking the end of the argument list.

This completes the description of the base classes. The classes in the
following sections are defined as derivations of Line, Text, Ruler, and two
derived classes.

_____Ruler.cc_____

```
#include "Ruler.h"


Ruler::Ruler ()
{
    lMargin = 0;
    rMargin = maxRMargin;
    for (int i = 0; i < 10; ++i)
        tabs[i] = (i+1) * 8;
    indent = leftInd;
} /* Ruler */


void
Ruler::Margins (short lMarg, short rMarg)
{
    lMargin = lMarg;
    rMargin = rMarg;
} /* Margins */


void
Ruler::Tabs (short tab1 ...)
{
    va_list args;
    short   tab = tab1;
    int     i = 0;
    va_start (args, tab1);
    do {
        tabs[i++] = tab;
    } while ((tab = va_arg(args, short)) != 0 && i < 10);
    va_end (args);
} /* Tabs */
```

13.3 Buffer and Script

The Buffer class is derived from Ruler; it provides buffer area and operations for formatting text. The static member buf is an array of buffer lines denoted by BufLine. Each line consists of a data field for storing the line, a len field which denotes the length of the line, and nWords which denotes the number of words in the line. The static member line is an index to the current line in buf.

Buffer::Buffer ()
The constructor initializes every line in buf to empty.

Bool Buffer::PutWord (char* word)
PutWord writes word to the current line in buf. If the word does not fit in the current line then it is written to the next line. A new line always begins with lMargin spaces. When word is longer than the line it is broken into two parts. All words are separated by a space. A line is always null-terminated. PutWord returns true if and only if word is successfully written.

_____Buffer.h_____

```
#ifndef _BUFFER_
#define _BUFFER_
#include "Consts.h"
#include "Ruler.h"
#include <string.h>

class Buffer : public virtual Ruler {
    struct BufLine {
        short   len;                    // length of the line
        short   nWords;                 // number of words in the line
        char    data[maxRMargin+2];     // line data
    };
    static  BufLine buf[bufLines];      // buffer area
    static  short line;                 // the current line
    void    IndentLine (short line);
public:
            Buffer      ();
    Bool    PutWord     (char* word);
    void    IndentText ();
    int     BufLines    ()                  { return line; }
    const   char* operator [] (short line);
};
#endif _BUFFER_
```

_____Buffer.cc_____

```
#include "Buffer.h"

Buffer::Buffer ()
{
    for (int i = 0; i < bufLines; ++i) {
        buf[i].len = buf[i].nWords = 0;
        buf[i].data[0] = '\0';
    }
    line = 0;
} /* Buffer */

Bool
Buffer::PutWord (char* word)
{
    int len = strlen(word);

    if (buf[line].len + len > rMargin) {              // not enough room?
        if (line < bufLines-1) {
            ++line;
            buf[line].nWords = buf[line].len = 0;
        } else
            return false;                             // buffer is full
    }
    if (buf[line].nWords == 0 && lMargin > 0) {   // build left margin
        for (int i = 0; i < lMargin; ++i)
            buf[line].data[i] = ' ';
        buf[line].len = lMargin;
    }
    if (len > rMargin - lMargin) {          // word longer than line, break it
        int  part = rMargin - buf[line].len;
        char save = word[part];
        word[part] = '\0';
        PutWord(word);                     // first half
        word[part] = save;
        return PutWord(word + part);       // second half
    }
    strncpy(buf[line].data + buf[line].len,word,len);
    buf[line].len += len;
    if (buf[line].len < rMargin)              // separate words with a space
        buf[line].data[buf[line].len++] = ' ';
    buf[line].data[len = buf[line].len] = '\0';
    buf[line].nWords++;
    return true;
} /* PutWord */
```

```
void
Buffer::IndentLine (short line)
{
    if (line < 0 || line > Buffer::line) return;
    int    width = rMargin - lMargin;
    int    gap = 0, lGap = 0, i;
    char* data = buf[line].data + lMargin;
    for (int left = lMargin; *data++ == ' '; ++left) ++gap;
    lGap = gap;
    data = buf[line].data + buf[line].len-1;
    for (int right = buf[line].len-1; *data-- == ' '; --right) ++gap;
    gap += rMargin - right;

    switch (indent) {
        case leftInd:
            data = buf[line].data + lMargin;
            for (i = 0; i <= right-left; ++i)         // shift left
                data[i] = data[lGap+i];
            data[i] = '\0';
            buf[line].len = lMargin + i;
            break;
        case centerInd:
            data = buf[line].data + lMargin;
            char temp[maxRMargin+2];
            for (i = 0; i <= right-left; ++i)         // copy to temp
                temp[i] = data[lGap+i];
            gap = gap / 2;
            for (i = 0; i < gap; ++i)                 // pad left
                data[i] = ' ';
            for (i = 0; i <= right-left; ++i)         // copy to data
                data[gap+i] = temp[i];
            data[gap+i] = '\0';
            buf[line].len = lMargin + gap + i;
            break;
        case rightInd:
            data = buf[line].data;
            data[buf[line].len = rMargin + 1] = '\0';
            int j = rMargin;
            for (i = right; i >= left; --i)           // shift right
                data[j--] = data[i];
            for (; j >= lMargin; --j)                 // pad left
                data[j] = ' ';
            break;
    } /* switch */
} /* IndentLine */
```

void Buffer::IndentLine (short line)
This function indents a line according to the indentation mode specified by the ruler. An index, left, is set to denote the first nonblank character in the line. Similarly, right is set to denote the last nonblank character in the line. The number of unused characters is denoted by gap (excluding the left margin blanks). LGap denotes the number of blanks on the left side of the line.

For left indentation, the line is left-shifted by lGap positions. For center indentation, the nonblank part of the line is first copied into temp, the line is left-padded with gap/2 spaces and then temp is copied back to the line. For right indentation, the line is right-shifted as far as the right margin and the vacant positions are filled with blanks. In all cases, the line is null-terminated. For simplicity, IndentLine ignores tabs.

void Buffer::IndentText ()
IndentText indents an entire text by calling IndentLine for every line.

const char* Buffer::operator [] (short line)
This operator returns the data part of the line denoted by line.

The Script class is derived from Text and Buffer. This class is used for formatting a piece of text. The private member formatted is set to true after the text has been formatted. Initially, it is set to false by the constructor.

void Script::Format ()
This function formats the text according to the ruler. To do so, Format first initializes the buffer by explicitly calling the Buffer constructor. It then copies the text to buffer by repeatedly calling GetWord and PutWord. Actual formatting is done by calling IndentText.

ostream& operator << (ostream& out, Script& scr)
If scr has not been formatted then << uses the overloaded << for Text. Otherwise, it outputs each line in the buffer using the default <<.

```
void
Buffer::IndentText ()
{
      for (int i = 0; i <= line; ++i) IndentLine(i);
} /* IndentText */

const char*
Buffer::operator [] (short line)
{
      return (line < 0 || line > Buffer::line) ? 0 : buf[line].data;
} /* operator [] */
```

_____Script.h_____

```
#ifndef _SCRIPT_
#define _SCRIPT_
#include "Text.h"
#include "Buffer.h"
#include <stream.h>

class Script : public virtual Text, public Buffer {
    Bool formatted;                             // true if text formatted
public:
            Script      ()       { formatted = false; }
    virtual void Format ();
    friend  ostream& operator << (ostream& out,Script& scr);
};
#endif _SCRIPT_
```

_____Script.cc_____

```
#include "Script.h"

void
Script::Format ()
{
    char word[maxWordSize+1];
    Buffer();                                   // initialize buffer
    while (GetWord(word) && PutWord(word))      // copy words to buffer
        ;
    IndentText();                               // indent text in buffer
    formatted = true;
} /* Format */

ostream&
operator << (ostream& out,Script& scr)
{
    if (!scr.formatted)
        out << (Text&) scr;                     // output raw text
    else
        for (int i = 0; i <= scr.BufLines(); ++i)
            out << scr[i] << "\n";              // output formatted text
} /* operator << */
```

13.4 Grid and Table

The Grid class is derived from Ruler and is used for arranging the words in a text
into a 2-dimensional grid. Like Buffer, all data members of this class are static.
Grid is very similar to Matrix (Chapter 5), except that its elements are all strings.
The maximum width of strings in each column is recorded in width.

Grid::Grid (short rows, short cols)
The constructor sets the grid to be of size rows and cols, and initializes all grid
elements to empty.

Bool Grid::PutElem (const char* elem)
PutElem inserts elem into the grid at the current row and column position.
Elements larger than maxItem are chopped. All elements are null-terminated. The
width array is updated if the element is longer than earlier ones in the same
column. PuElem returns true if and only if elem is successfully inserted.

const char* Grid::operator () (short row, short col)
Overloaded () is used for retrieving a grid element. Before returning it, an
element is formatted according to the ruler. If the element is in the first column
then it is left-padded with lMargin blank spaces. For simplicity, () ignores tabs.

```
                              Grid.h
#ifndef _GRID_
#define _GRID_
#include "Consts.h"
#include "Ruler.h"
#include <string.h>

class Grid : public virtual Ruler {
     static  short rows;                  // number of rows
     static  short cols;                  // number of columns
     static  short row;                   // current row
     static  short col;                   // current column
     static  char  elems[maxRows][maxCols][maxItem];   // grid elements
     static  short width[maxCols];        // maximum width of each column
public:
             Grid           (short rows, short cols);
     Bool    PutElem        (const char* elem);
     const   char* operator () (short row, short col);
};
#endif _GRID_
```

The margin boundaries for indenting an element are decided by the boundaries of each column which are in turn decided by the width of the column. The result of indentation is copied to a local static buffer, null-terminated, and then returned.

_____Grid.cc_____

```
#include "Grid.h"

Grid::Grid (short rows,short cols)
{
    Grid::rows = rows > maxRows ? maxRows : rows;
    Grid::cols = cols > maxCols ? maxCols : cols;
    row = col = 0;
    for (int c = 0; c < maxCols; ++c) {
        width[c] = 0;
        for (int r = 0; r < maxRows; ++r)
            elems[r][c][0] = '\0';
    }
} /* Grid */

Bool
Grid::PutElem (const char* elem)
{
    if (col == cols) {
        if (row == rows)
            return false;                              // grid is full
        ++row;
        col = 0;
    }
    int len = strlen(elem);

    if (len >= maxItem) {                              // too long?
        strncpy(elems[row][col],elem,len = maxItem - 1);
        elems[row][col][maxItem-1] = '\0';             // chop it
    } else
        strcpy(elems[row][col],elem);
    if (len > width[col])                              // update 'width'
        width[col] = len;
    ++col;
    return true;
} /* PutElem */
```

```
const char*
Grid::operator () (short row, short col)
{
    static char buffer[maxRMargin+1];
    char*  buf = buffer;
    row = row >= rows ? rows-1 : row;
    col = col >= cols ? cols-1 : col;
    const char* data = elems[row][col];
    int   i;

    if (col == 0) {
        for (i = 0; i < lMargin; ++i)                 // pad left margin
            buf[i] = ' ';
        buf[i] = '\0';
        buf += i;
    }
    int len = strlen(data);

    switch (indent) {
        case leftInd:
            strcpy(buf,data);
            for (i = len; i < width[col]; ++i)        // pad right
                buf[i] = ' ';
            break;
        case centerInd:
            for (i = 0; i < (width[col]-len)/2; ++i)  // pad left
                buf[i] = ' ';
            strcpy(buf + i,data);
            for (i += len; i < width[col]; ++i)       // pad right
                buf[i] = ' ';
            break;
        case rightInd:
            for (i = 0; i < width[col] - len; ++i)    // pad left
                buf[i] = ' ';
            strcpy(buf + i,data);
            i += len;
            break;
    } /* switch */

    buf[i] = '\0';
    return buffer;
} /* operator () */
```

The `Table` class is derived from `Text` and `Grid`. It is used for formatting text in tabular form. The dimensions of the table are denoted by `rows` and `cols`. The gap between the table columns is denoted by `gap`. `Formatted` is set to true after a table has been formatted.

Table::Table (short rows, short cols, short gap = 1)
The constructor sets the dimensions of the table and the gap between the columns. All tables are initially unformatted.

void Table::Format ()
This function formats a piece of text into a table. To do so, `Format` copies the text to a grid by repeatedly calling `GetWord` and `PutElem`.

ostream& operator << (ostream& out, Table& tab)
If `tab` has not been formatted then `<<` uses the overloaded `<<` for `Text`. Otherwise, it outputs the table row by row. A string of `gap` blank spaces is built in `gapBuf`. Each row is output element by element and `gapBuf` is output after each element.

```
_____Table.h_____
#ifndef _TABLE_
#define _TABLE_
#include "Text.h"
#include "Grid.h"
#include <stream.h>

class Table : public virtual Text, public Grid {
        short    rows;                  // table rows
        short    cols;                  // table columns
        short    gap;                   // gap between columns
        Bool     formatted;             // true if table formatted
public:
                 Table       (short rows, short cols, short gap = 1);
        virtual void Format ();
        friend  ostream& operator << (ostream& out, Table& par);
};
#endif _TABLE_
```

_____Table.cc_____

```cpp
#include "Table.h"

Table::Table (short rows, short cols, short gap) : Grid(rows, cols)
{
    Table::rows = rows > maxRows ? maxRows : rows;
    Table::cols = cols > maxCols ? maxCols : cols;
    Table::gap = gap > maxItem ? maxItem : gap;
    formatted = false;
} /* Table */

void
Table::Format ()
{
    char word[maxWordSize+1];
    while (GetWord(word) && PutElem(word))      // copy words to grid
        ;
    formatted = true;
} /* Format */

ostream&
operator << (ostream& out, Table& tab)
{
    if (!tab.formatted)                          // output raw text
        out << (Text&) tab;
    else {                                       // output formatted table
        char gapBuf[maxItem+1];

        for (int i = 0; i < tab.gap; ++i)        // build gap string
            gapBuf[i] = ' ';
        gapBuf[i] = '\0';

        for (int r = 0; r < tab.rows; ++r) {     // output rows
            for (int c = 0; c < tab.cols; ++c)
                out << tab(r,c) << gapBuf;
            out << "\n";
        }
    }
} /* operator << */
```

13.5 Paragraph

We would like to regard both Script and Table as variations of a more general class – a Paragraph. To do so, we derive Paragraph from Script and Table. It contains only one data member, kind, which indicates whether the paragraph is a script or a table. This is set by the constructor.

Format and overloaded << simply call the corresponding functions from Script and Table.

```
                              Paragraph.h
#ifndef _PARAGRAPH_
#define _PARAGRAPH_
#include "Script.h"
#include "Table.h"

class Paragraph : public Script, public Table {
    ParKind kind;
public:
    Paragraph      (ParKind kd, short rows = 0, short cols = 0);
    void    Format ();
    friend ostream& operator << (ostream& out, Paragraph& par);
};
#endif _PARAGRAPH_
```

```
                              Paragraph.cc
#include "Paragraph.h"

Paragraph::Paragraph (ParKind kd, short rows, short cols)
  : Table (rows, col)           { kind = kd; }

void
Paragraph::Format ()
{
    if (kind == script)
        Script::Format ();
    else
        Table::Format ();
} /* Format */

ostream&
operator << (ostream& out, Paragraph& par)
{
    return par.kind == script
                ? out << (Script&) par
                : out << (Table&) par;
} /* operator << */
```

13.6 Concluding remarks

The development of the above classes has been strictly bottom-up. We started with very simple classes, such as `Line`, and `Ruler`, and gradually produced more complicated, larger classes. The resulting class hierarchy is shown in Figure 13.1.

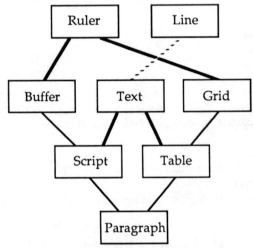

Figure 13.1 Class hierarchy. Thick lines denote virtual base classes.
The dotted line denotes member object.

We could also have taken a top-down approach by starting with an abstract class such as `Paragraph` and deriving less abstract classes, such as `Script` and `Table`, from it. This would have resulted in a totally different class hierarchy. Alternatively, we could have taken a middle-out approach and started with a class such as `Text`.

The fact that, for a given problem, many different class hierarchies are possible is an indication of the richness of the object-oriented approach. Proper object-oriented design requires the investigation and comparison of these design alternatives to decide which is more appropriate.

Our word processing program is by no means complete. Only a skimmed version of most of the classes has been presented. Other operations need to be added to these classes before they can be used in a realistic word processor. Other classes also need to be defined. For example, we need classes for representing sections and chapters. We conclude this chapter by sketching the declarations of these two. Their implementation is left as an exercise.

```
class Section {
        short secNo;          // section number
        short nParag;         // number of allocated paragraphs
        short used;           // number of used paragraphs
        Paragraph* pars;      // vector of paragraph pointers
        Section* parent;      // parent section
        Section* subs;        // subsections
        Section* next;        // next section (linked-list)
public:
        //...
};

class Chapter {
        File file;            // chapter file
        short chapNo;         // chapter number
        Paragraph title;      // chapter title
        Section* first;       // first section
public:
        //...
};
```

13.7 Summary

Units of composition in a word processor (e.g., line, paragraph) are easily represented by classes. In this way, larger units can be composed out of smaller units.

A **bottom-up** approach to object-oriented programming starts with the lowest level classes and gradually produces more complicated classes by combining these.

A **top-down** approach starts with the highest level classes and successively decomposes these into smaller classes.

Object-oriented programming is often practiced as a **middle-out** approach. This is a hybrid of the bottom-up and the top-down approach.

Solutions to Exercises

1.1

```
class Set {
      int elems[maxCard];
      int card;
public:
      int Card ()                     { return card; }
      //...
};
```

1.2

```
void
Set::Intersect (Set* set,Set* res)    // find the intersection of two sets
{
      res->card = 0;                  // res initially empty
      for (int i = 0; i < card; ++i)
            // we could call Member instead of the next loop:
            for (int j = 0; j < set->card; ++j)
                  if (elems[i] == set->elems[j]) {
                        res->elems[res->card++] = elems[i];
                        break;
                  }
} /* Intersect */


ErrCode
Set::Union (Set* set,Set* res)        // find the union of two sets
{
      set->Copy(res);
      for (int i = 0; i < card; ++i)
            if (res->AddElem(elems[i]) == overflow)
                  return overflow;
      return noErr;
} /* Union */
```

1.3

```
class Set {
    //...
public:
    //...
    Bool Subset (Set*);
    Bool PSubset (Set* set)    { return card < set->card && Subset(set); }
};


Bool
Set::Subset (Set* set)                  // test if a set is a subset of another
{
    if (card > set->card)
        return false;
    for (int i = 0; i < card; ++i)
        if (!set->Member(elems[i]))
            return false;
    return true;
} /* Subset */
```

2.1

```
Bool
SymTable::RmvSym (char* name)
{
    int slot = Hash(name);
    Symbol* sym = table[slot];
    if (sym && strcmp(sym->name,name) == 0) {              // front of list
        table[slot] = sym->next;
        delete sym;
        return true;
    }
    for (sym = table[slot]; sym->next; sym = sym->next)   // rest of list
        if (strcmp(sym->next->name,name) == 0) {
            Symbol* tmp = sym->next;
            sym->next = sym->next->next;
            delete tmp;
            return true;
        }
    return false;
} /* RmvSym */
```

2.2

```
Bool
SymTable::SetValue (char* name,SymValue val)
{
    Symbol* sym = FindSym(name);
    if (sym == 0) return AddSym(name,val) != 0;
    else sym->value = val;
    return true;
} /* SetValue */

Bool
SymTable::GetValue (char* name,SymValue* val)
{
    Symbol* sym = FindSym(name);
    if (sym != 0) *val = sym->value;
    return sym != 0;
} /* GetValue */
```

2.3

```
#include <stream.h>

enum Bool {false,true};
struct BinNode {
    int value;
    BinNode* left;
    BinNode* right;
};

class BinTree {
    BinNode* root;
    Bool ok;                // set to true if operation successful
    void      FreeBinNode (BinNode* node);
    BinNode* InsertNode (BinNode* node,BinNode* tree);
    BinNode* DeleteNode (int val,BinNode* tree);
    void      PrintNode (BinNode* node);
public:
        BinTree ()          { root = 0; }
        ~BinTree ()         { FreeBinNode(root); }
    Bool Insert (int val);
    Bool Delete (int val);
    void Print ()           { PrintNode(root);  cout << "\n"; }
};
```

```cpp
void
BinTree::FreeBinNode (BinNode* node)
{
    if (node != 0) {
        FreeBinNode(node->left);
        FreeBinNode(node->right);
        delete node;
    }
} /* FreeBinNode */


BinNode*
BinTree::InsertNode (BinNode* node,BinNode* tree)
{
    if (tree == 0) return node;
    if (node->value < tree->value)
        tree->left = InsertNode(node,tree->left);
    else if (node->value > tree->value)
        tree->right = InsertNode(node,tree->right);
    else
        delete node;                    // already there
    return tree;
} /* IndertNode */


BinNode*
BinTree::DeleteNode (int val,BinNode* tree)
{
    if (tree == 0) return tree;
    if (val < tree->value)
        tree->left = DeleteNode(val,tree->left);
    else if (val > tree->value)
        tree->right = DeleteNode(val,tree->right);
    else {
        BinNode* temp = tree;
        if (tree->left == 0)
            tree = tree->right;
        else if (tree->right == 0)
            tree = tree->left;
        else
            tree = InsertNode(tree->left,tree->right);
        ok = true;
        delete temp;
    }
    return tree;
} /* DeleteNode */
```

```
void
BinTree::PrintNode (BinNode* node)
{
    if (node != 0) {
        PrintNode(node->left);
        cout << node->value<< "  ";
        PrintNode(node->right);
    }
} /* PrintNode */

Bool
BinTree::Insert (int val)
{
    BinNode* node = new BinNode;
    ok = false;
    if (node != 0) {
        node->value = val;
        node->left = node->right = 0;
        root = InsertNode(node,root);
    }
    return ok;
} /* Insert */

Bool
BinTree::Delete (int val)
{
    ok = false;
    root = DeleteNode(val,root);
    return ok;
} /* Delete */
```

2.4

```
Symbol*
SymTable::AddSym (char* name,SymValue value)
{
    Symbol* sym;
    int slot = Hash(name);

    if ((sym = new Symbol) != 0 &&
        (sym->name = new char[strlen(name)+1]) != 0) {
        strcpy(sym->name,name);
```

```
        sym->value = value;
        if (table[slot] == 0 || strcmp(name,table[slot]->name) < 0) {
            sym->next = table[slot];   // insert in front
            table[slot] = sym;
        } else {
            Symbol* s = table[slot];
            while (s->next && strcmp(name,s->next->name) > 0) s = s->next;
            sym->next = s->next;         // insert in tail
            s->next = sym;
        }
        return sym;
    } else {
        delete sym;
        sym = 0;
    }
    return sym;
} /* AddSym */


Bool
SymTable::RmvSym (char* name)
{
    int slot = Hash(name);
    int cmp;
    Symbol* sym = table[slot];

    if (sym && strcmp(sym->name,name) == 0) {  // in front of list
        table[slot] = sym->next;
        delete sym;
        return true;
    }
    for (sym = table[slot];
         sym->next && (cmp = strcmp(name,sym->name)) >= 0;
         sym = sym->next)
        if (cmp == 0) {
            Symbol* tmp = sym->next;
            sym->next = sym->next->next;
            delete tmp;
            return true;
        }
    return false;
} /* RmvSym */
```

```
Symbol*
SymTable::FindSym (char* name)
{
    int slot = Hash(name);
    int cmp;
    for (Symbol* sym = table[slot];
            sym && (cmp = strcmp(name,sym->name)) >= 0;
            sym = sym->next)
        if (cmp == 0) return sym;
    return 0;
} /* FindSym */
```

3.1

```
Sequence::Sequence (BinaryTree* tree)
{
    items = new int[size = tree->TreeSize()];
    used = 0;
    MakeSeq(tree->root,this);
} /* Sequence */

void MakeSeq (Node* node,Sequence* seq)
{
    if (node->left)
        MakeSeq(node->left,seq);
    seq->items[seq->used++] = node->item;
    if (node->right)
        MakeSeq(node->right,seq);
} /* MakeSeq */
```

3.2

```
BinaryTree::BinaryTree(Sequence* seq,int low = 0,int high = 0)
{
    if (low == 0 && high == 0)
        high = seq->used;
    root = (low < 0 || high < 0 || low > seq->used || high > seq->used)
                ? 0
                : MakeTree(seq,low,high);
} /* BinaryTree */
```

```
Node*
MakeTree (Sequence* seq, int low, int high)
{
    int mid = (low + high) / 2;
    Node* node = new Node;
    if (node != 0) {
        if (low < high) {                           // increasing order
            node->left = (mid == low ? 0 : MakeTree(seq,low,mid-1));
            node->right = (mid == high ? 0 : MakeTree(seq,mid+1,high));
        } else if (low > high) {                    // decreasing order
            node->left  = (mid == low ? 0 : MakeTree(seq,low,mid+1));
            node->right = (mid == high ? 0 : MakeTree(seq,mid-1,high));
        }
        node->item = seq->items[mid];
    }
    return node;
} /* MakeTree */
```

3.3

```
ErrCode
Set::Union (Set* set, Set* res)
{
    set->Copy(res);
    for (int i = 0; i < this->card; ++i)
        if (res->AddElem(this->elems[i]) == overflow) return overflow;
    return noErr;
} /* Union */
```

4.1

```
overload Max;
int     Max (int x, int y)            { return x > y ? x : y; }
double Max (double x, double y)       { return x > y ? x : y; }
char*  Max (char* x, char* y)         { return strcmp(x,y) > 0 ? x : y; }
```

4.2

```
Set operator + (Set set1, Set set2)
{
    Set res = set1;
    for (int i = 0; i < set2.card; ++i)
        res.AddElem(set2.elems[i]);
    return res;
} /* operator + */
```

```
Bool operator < (Set set1, Set set2)
{
    return set1.card < set2.card && set1 <= set2;
} /* operator < */

Bool operator <= (Set set1, Set set2)
{
    if (set1.card > set2.card) return false;
    for (int i = 0; i < set1.card; ++i)
        if (!(set1.elems[i] & set2)) return false;
    return true;
} /* operator <= */
```

4.3

```
Binary operator - (Binary n1, Binary n2)
{
    unsigned borrow = 0;
    int    value;
    Binary res = "0";
    for (int i = 15; i >= 0; --i) {
        value = (n1.bits[i] == '0' ? 0 : 1) -
                (n2.bits[i] == '0' ? 0 : 1) + borrow;
        res.bits[i] = (value == -1 || value == 1 ? '1': '0');
        borrow = (value == -1 || borrow != 0 && value == 1 ? 1 : 0);
    }
    return(res);
} /* operator - */
```

4.4

```
#include <stream.h>

class Matrix {
    //...
};

Matrix::Matrix (short rows, short cols)
{
    Matrix::rows = rows;
    Matrix::cols = cols;
    elems = new double[rows * cols];
} /* Matrix */
```

```
inline
Matrix::~Matrix ()       { delete elems; }

double
Matrix::operator () (short row,short col)
{
    return (row >= 1 && row <= rows && col >= 1 && col <= cols)
            ? elems[(row - 1)*cols + (col - 1)];
            : 0.0;
} /* operator () */

void
Matrix::SetElem (short row,short col,double val)
{
    if (row >= 1 && row <= rows && col >= 1 && col <= cols)
        elems[(row - 1)*cols + (col - 1)] = val;
} /* SetElem */

Matrix
operator + (Matrix p,Matrix q)
{
    Matrix m(p.rows,p.cols);
    if (p.rows != q.rows || p.cols != q.cols)      // mismatch
        return m;
    for (int r = 1; r <= p.rows; ++r)
        for (int c = 1; c <= p.cols; ++c)
            m.SetElem(r,c,p(r,c) + q(r,c));
    return m;
} /* operator + */

Matrix
operator - (Matrix p,Matrix q)
{
    Matrix m(p.rows,p.cols);
    if (p.rows != q.rows || p.cols != q.cols)      // mismatch
        return m;
    for (int r = 1; r <= p.rows; ++r)
        for (int c = 1; c <= p.cols; ++c)
            m.SetElem(r,c,p(r,c) - q(r,c));
    return m;
} /* operator - */
```

```
Matrix
operator * (Matrix p,Matrix q)
{
    Matrix m(p.rows,q.cols);
    if (p.cols != q.rows)                            // mismatch
        return m;
    for (int r = 1; r <= p.rows; ++r)
        for (int c = 1; c <= q.cols; ++c) {
            m.SetElem(r,c,0.0);
            for (int i = 1; i <= p.cols; ++i)
                m.SetElem(r,c,m(r,c) + p(r,c) * q(r,c));
        }
    return m;
} /* operator * */


void
Matrix::Print ()
{
    for (int r = 1; r <= rows; ++r) {
        for (int c = 1; c <= cols; ++c)
            cout << form("%6.2f ",(*this)(r,c));
        cout << "\n";
    }
    cout << "\n";
} /* Print */
```

5.1

```
BitVec::BitVec (short dim)
{
    dim = dim <= 0 ? 8 : dim;
    bytes = dim / 8 + (dim % 8 == 0 ? 0 : 1);
    vec = (unsigned char*) new char[bytes];

    for (int i = 0; i < bytes; ++i)
            vec[i] = 0;                              // all bits are initially zero
} /* BitVec */


BitVec::BitVec (char* bits)
{
    int len = strlen(bits);
    bytes = len / 8 + (len % 8 == 0 ? 0 : 1);
    vec = (unsigned char*) new char[bytes];
```

```
    for (int i = 0; i < bytes; ++i)
        vec[i] = 0;                          // initialize all bits to zero
    for (i = len - 1; i >= 0; --i)
        if (*bits++ == '1')                  // set the 1 bits
            vec[i/8] |= (1 << (i%8));
} /* BitVec */


inline Bool
BitVec::operator [] (short idx)         // return the bit denoted by idx
{
    return vec[idx/8] & (1 << idx%8) ? true : false;
} /* operator [] */


inline void
BitVec::Set (short idx)                 // set the bit denoted by idx to 1
{
    vec[idx/8] |= (1 << idx%8);
} /* Set */


inline void
BitVec::Reset (short idx)               // reset the bit denoted by idx to 0
{
    vec[idx/8] &= ~(1 << idx%8);
} /* Reset */


BitVec
operator ~ (BitVec& v)                  // bitwise COMPLEMENT of v
{
    BitVec r(v.bytes * 8);
    for (int i = 0; i < v.bytes; ++i)
        r.vec[i] = ~v.vec[i];
    return r;
} /* operator ~ */


BitVec
operator & (BitVec& v, BitVec& w)       // bitwise AND of v and w
{
    BitVec r((v.bytes > w.bytes ? v.bytes : w.bytes) * 8);
    for (int i = 0; i < (v.bytes < w.bytes ? v.bytes : w.bytes); ++i)
        r.vec[i] = v.vec[i] & w.vec[i];
    return r;
} /* operator & */
```

```
BitVec
operator | (BitVec& v,BitVec& w)        // bitwise OR of v and w
{
    BitVec r((v.bytes > w.bytes ? v.bytes : w.bytes) * 8);
    for (int i = 0; i < (v.bytes < w.bytes ? v.bytes : w.bytes); ++i)
        r.vec[i] = v.vec[i] | w.vec[i];
    return r;
} /* operator | */


BitVec
operator ^ (BitVec& v,BitVec& w)        // bitwise exclusive-OR of v and w
{
    BitVec r((v.bytes > w.bytes ? v.bytes : w.bytes) * 8);
    for (int i = 0; i < (v.bytes < w.bytes ? v.bytes : w.bytes); ++i)
        r.vec[i] = v.vec[i] ^ w.vec[i];
    return r;
} /* operator ^ */


BitVec
operator << (BitVec& v,short n)        // SHIFT v LEFT by n bits
{
    BitVec r(v.bytes * 8);
    int zeros = n / 8;      // bytes on the left to become zero
    int shift = n % 8;      // left shift for remaining bytes
    int i;

    for (i = v.bytes - 1; i >= zeros; --i)   // shift bytes left
        r.vec[i] = v.vec[i - zeros];

    for (; i >= 0; --i)                        // zero left bytes
        r.vec[i] = 0;
    unsigned char prev = 0;

    for (i = zeros; i < r.bytes; ++i) {        // shift bits left
        r.vec[i] = (r.vec[i] << shift) | prev;
        prev = v.vec[i - zeros] >> (8 - shift);
    }
    return r;
} /* operator << */
```

```
BitVec
operator >> (BitVec& v,short n)        // SHIFT v RIGHT by n bits
{
    BitVec r(v.bytes * 8);
    int zeros = n / 8;                 // bytes on the right to become zero
    int shift = n % 8;                 // right shift for remaining bytes
    int i;
    for (i = 0; i < v.bytes - zeros; ++i)     // shift bytes right
        r.vec[i] = v.vec[i + zeros];
    for (; i < v.bytes; ++i)           // zero right bytes
        r.yec[i] = 0;
    unsigned char prev = 0;
    for (i = r.bytes - zeros - 1; i >= 0; --i) {
    // shift bits right
        r.vec[i] = (r.vec[i] >> shift) | prev;
        prev = v.vec[i + zeros] << (8 - shift);
    }
    return r;
} /* operator >> */


Bool
operator == (BitVec& v,BitVec& w)          // test for EQUALITY of v and w
{
    int smaller = v.bytes < w.bytes ? v.bytes : w.bytes;
    for (int i = 0; i < smaller; ++i)     // compare bytes
        if (v.vec[i] != w.vec[i])
            return false;
    for (i = smaller; i < v.bytes; ++i) // extra bytes in v
        if (v.vec[i] != 0)
            return false;
    for (i = smaller; i < w.bytes; ++i) // extra bytes in w
        if (w.vec[i] != 0)
            return false;
    return true;
} /* operator == */


inline Bool
operator != (BitVec& v,BitVec& w)          // test for INEQUALITY of v and w
{
    return !(v == w);
} /* operator != */
```

5.2

```
Matrix operator * (Matrix& p,Matrix& q)
{
    Matrix m(p.rows,q.cols);

    for (Element* pe = p.elems; pe != 0; pe = pe->next)
        for (Element* qe = q.elems; qe != 0; qe = qe->next)
            if (pe->col == qe->row)
                m(pe->row,qe->col) += pe->val * qe->val;
    return m;
} /* operator * */
```

5.3

```
Matrix::~Matrix ()
{
    Element* elem = elems;
    Element* tmp;

    while (elem != 0) {
        tmp = elem;
        elem = elem->next;
        delete tmp;
    }
} /* ~Matrix */
```

5.4

No, because the [] operator requires a pointer type.

6.1

```
class SymTable {                         // base class
    Symbol** table;
    int      size;
    int      Hash (char*);
public:
                    SymTable (int);
    virtual Symbol* AddSym (char*,SymValue);
    virtual Symbol* FindSym (char*);
    virtual Bool    RmvSym (char*);
            void    PrintTable ();
};
```

```
class SSymTable : public SymTable { // derived class
public:
    Symbol* AddSym (char*,SymValue);
    Symbol* FindSym (char*);
    Bool    RmvSym (char*);
};
```

The private part of SymTable should be declared as protected, or SSymTable should be declared a friend of SymTable. The definition of the new member functions is the same as those given in Solution 2.3.

6.2

```
class SSymTable : public SymTable {
public:
    SSymTable (int sz,int sig) : (sz)    { sigChars = sig; }
    //...
};
```

6.3

```
// Solves the equations by reducing the augmented matrix m to the upper-
// triangular form using partial pivot search and guassian elimination
void
LinEqns::Solve ()
{
    double const epsilon = 1e-5;
    double temp;
    int diag, piv, r, c;

    for (diag = 1; diag <= nEqns; ++diag) {
        piv = diag;
        for (r = diag+1; r <= nEqns; ++r)
            if (abs((*this)(piv,diag)) < abs((*this)(r,diag)))
                piv = r;
        // make sure there is a unique solution:
        if (abs((*this)(piv,diag)) < epsilon) {
            if (abs((*this)(diag,nEqns+1)) < epsilon)
                cout << "infinite solutions\n";
            else
                cout << "no solution\n";
            return;
        }
```

```
        if (piv != diag)
            for (c = 1; c <= nEqns+1; ++c) {
                temp = (*this) (diag,c);
                (*this) (diag,c) = (*this) (piv,c);
                (*this) (piv,c) = temp;
            }

        // normalise diag row so that m[diag,diag] = 1:
        temp = (*this) (diag,diag);
        (*this) (diag,diag) = 1.0;
        for (c = diag+1; c <= nEqns+1; ++c)
            (*this) (diag,c) = (*this) (diag,c) / temp;

        // now eliminate entries below the pivot:
        for (r = diag+1; r <= nEqns; ++r) {
            double factor = (*this) (r,diag);
            (*this) (r,diag) = 0.0;
            for (c = diag+1; c <= nEqns+1; ++c)
                (*this) (r,c) -= (*this) (diag,c) * factor;
        }
        cout << "eliminated below pivot in column " << diag << "\n";
        Print();
    }

    // back substitute:
    double* soln = new double[nEqns];
    soln[nEqns-1] = (*this) (nEqns,nEqns+1);
    // the last unknown

    for (r = nEqns-1; r >= 1; --r) {          // the rest
        double sum = 0.0;
        for (diag = r+1; diag <= nEqns; ++diag)
            sum += (*this) (r,diag) * soln[diag-1];
        soln[r-1] = (*this) (r,nEqns+1) - sum;
    }
    for (r = 1; r <= nEqns; ++r)
        cout << "        x[" << r << "] = " << soln[r-1] << "\n";
    delete soln;
} /* Solve */
```

7.1

```
class BitMap {                                      // base class
    //...
public:
    BitMap (int rows,int cols);
};

class TextEdit {                                    // base class
    //...
public:
    TextEdit (char* text);
};

class Icon : public BitMap, public TextEdit {       // derived class
    //...
public:
    Icon (char* name);
};

Icon::Icon (char* name) : BitMap(16,16), TextEdit(name)
{   //...
}
```

7.2

```
class Window {                      // base class
    Rectangle bounds;
    char*      contents;
public:
    Window (Rectangle bounds);
    //...
};

class Menu {                        // base class
    Option* options;
    Menu*   owner;
public:
    Menu (Menu* owner);
    //...
};
```

```
class MenuWindow : Window {            // derived class
    Menu*    m;
    Option*  curOptn;
    MenuKind kind;
public:
    MenuWindow (MenuKind,Menu*,Rectangle);
    //...
};


MenuWindow::MenuWindow (MenuKind kind,Menu* owner,Rectangle bounds)
: (bounds), m(owner)
{    //...
}
```

8.1

```
inline BitVec&
BitVec::operator &= (BitVec& v)
    // (*this) &= v;
{
    return (*this) = (*this) & v;
} /* operator &= */

inline BitVec&
BitVec::operator |= (BitVec& v)
    // (*this) |= v;
{
    return (*this) = (*this) | v;
} /* operator |= */

inline BitVec&
BitVec::operator ^= (BitVec& v)
    // (*this) ^= v;
{
    return (*this) = (*this) ^ v;
} /* operator ^= */

inline BitVec&
BitVec::operator <<= (short n)
    // (*this) <<= v;
{
    return (*this) = (*this) << n;
} /* operator <<= */
```

```
inline BitVec&
BitVec::operator >>= (short n)
    // (*this) >>= v;
{
    return (*this) = (*this) >> n;
} /* operator >>= */
```

8.2

```
inline EnumSet
operator - (EnumSet& s,EnumSet& t)
{
    return s & ~t;
} /* operator - */
```

```
inline EnumSet
operator * (EnumSet& s,EnumSet& t)
{
    return s & t;
} /* operator * */
```

```
inline Bool
operator % (short elem,EnumSet& t)
{
    return t[elem];
} /* operator + */
```

```
inline Bool
operator <= (EnumSet& s,EnumSet& t)
{
    return (t & s) == s;
} /* operator <= */
```

```
inline Bool
operator >= (EnumSet& s,EnumSet& t)
{
    return (t & s) == t;
} /* operator >= */
```

```
EnumSet&
operator << (EnumSet& s,short elem)
{
    s.Set(elem);
    return s;
} /* operator << */

EnumSet&
operator >> (EnumSet& s,short elem)
{
    s.Reset(elem);
    return s;
} /* operator >> */
```

9.1

```
#include <stream.h>
#include <stdarg.h>

const bufSize = 128;
void PrintF (char* format ...)
{
    va_list args;
    char buf[bufSize];
    int  bufIdx = 0;
    va_start(args,format);
    while (*format != '\0' && bufIdx < bufSize-1) {
       if (*format == '%') {
          if (bufIdx > 0) {
             buf[bufIdx] = '\0';
             cout << buf;
             bufIdx = 0;
          }
          switch (*++format) {
             case 'd': cout << va_arg(args,int);       // %d
                       break;
             case 'f': cout << va_arg(args,double);  // %f
                       break;
             case 's': cout << va_arg(args,char*);   // %s
                       break;
             default:  buf[bufIdx++] = *format;       // ignore %
                       break;
          }
```

```
            ++format;
        } else
            buf[bufIdx++] = *format++;
    }
    va_end(args);
    if (bufIdx > 0) {                        // make sure buf is empty
        buf[bufIdx] = 0;
        cout << buf;
    }
} /* PrintF */
```

9.2

```
#include <stream.h>
#include <stdarg.h>

const maxOptions = 32;
typedef void (*Action)(void);

int Menu (char* option1,Action act1 ...)
{
    va_list args;
    char*    option = option1;
    int      count = 0, choice = 0;
    Action   acts[maxOptions];
    acts[count] = act1;
    va_start(args,act1);
    for (;;) {
        cout << ++count << ". " << option << "\n";
        if ((option = va_arg(args,char*)) == 0)
            break;
        acts[count] = va_arg(args,Action);   // save the action in acts
    }
    va_end(args);
    cout << "option? ";
    cin >> choice;
    if (choice > 0 && choice <= count) {
        if (acts[choice-1] != 0)       // do the action if not 0
            (*acts[choice-1])();
        return choice;
    }
    return -1;
} /* Menu */
```

Bibliography

Booch, G., 1986, Object-oriented development, *IEEE Transactions on Software Engineering*, vol. 12, no. 2, pp. 211-21.

Comer, D., 1979, *The Ubiquitous B-Tree*, Computing Surveys, vol. 11, no. 2, pp. 121-37.

Green, M., 1985, Design notations and user interface management systems, in *UIMS*, G. E. Pfaff (ed.), Springer-Verlag, Berlin.

Gehani, N. H., 1983, High level form definition in office information systems, *The Computer Journal*, vol. 26, no. 1, pp. 52-9.

Hekmatpour, S., 1989, A window manager for UNIX, *The Computer Journal*, vol. 32, no. 1, pp. 21-3.

Horowitz, E. and Sahni, S., 1987, *Data Structures in Pascal*, 2nd edition, Computer Science Press, Maryland.

Kernighan, B. W. and Ritchie, D. M., 1988, *The C Programming Language*, 2nd edition, Prentice Hall, Englewood Cliffs, NJ.

Lea, D., 1989, *User's Guide to GNU C++ Library*, Free Software Foundation, Inc.

Meyer, B., 1987, Reusability: the case for object-oriented design, *IEEE Software*, pp. 50-64.

Olsen Jr., D. R., 1983, Automatic generation of interactive systems, *ACM Computer Graphics*, vol. 17, no. 1, pp. 53-7.

Strang, G. and Fix, G., 1973, *An Analysis of Finite Element Method*, Prentice Hall, Englewood Cliffs, NJ.

Stroustrup, B., 1986, *The C++ Programming Language*, Addison-Wesley, Reading, MA.

Sutton, J. A. and Sprague, R. H., 1978, A study of display generation and management in interactive business applications, *IBM Research Report RJ2392*.

Tiemann, M. D., 1989, *User's Guide to GNU C++*, Free Software Foundation, Inc.

Verity, J. W., 1987, The OOPS Revolution, *DATAMATION*, pp. 73-8.

Watt, D. A., Wichmann, B. A. and Findlay, W., 1987, *Ada: Language and Methodology*, Prentice Hall, Hemel Hempstead.

Wiener, R. S., 1987, Object-oriented programming in C++ – a case study, *SIGPLAN Notices*, vol. 22, no. 6, pp. 59-68.

Index